Key Topics in Second Language Acquisition

MIX
Paper from
responsible sources
FSC
www.fsc.org   FSC® C013604

MM Textbooks

Key Topics in Second Language Acquisition

Vivian Cook and David Singleton

MULTILINGUAL MATTERS
Bristol • Buffalo • Toronto

Library of Congress Cataloging in Publication Data
A catalog record for this book is available from the Library of Congress.
Cook, Vivian, 1940-
Key Topics in Second Language Acquisition/Vivian Cook and David Singleton.
MM Textbooks: 10
Includes bibliographical references and index.
1. Second language acquisition. 2. Language and languages--Study and teaching.
I. Singleton, D. M. (David Michael) II. Title.
P118.2.C669 2014
401'.93–dc23 2013049006

British Library Cataloguing in Publication Data
A catalogue entry for this book is available from the British Library.

ISBN-13: 978-1-78309-180-5 (hbk)
ISBN-13: 978-1-78309-179-9 (pbk)

Multilingual Matters
UK: St Nicholas House, 31-34 High Street, Bristol BS1 2AW, UK.
USA: UTP, 2250 Military Road, Tonawanda, NY 14150, USA.
Canada: UTP, 5201 Dufferin Street, North York, Ontario M3H 5T8, Canada.

The policy of Multilingual Matters/Channel View Publications is to use papers that are natural, renewable and recyclable products, made from wood grown in sustainable forests. In the manufacturing process of our books, and to further support our policy, preference is given to printers that have FSC and PEFC Chain of Custody certification. The FSC and/or PEFC logos will appear on those books where full certification has been granted to the printer concerned.

Typeset by The Charlesworth Group.
Printed and bound in Great Britain by the CPI Group (UK Ltd), Croydon, CR0 4YY.

Contents

List of Boxes

Topic 4: How Important is Grammar in Acquiring and Using a Second Language?

Topic 5: How Do People Learn to Write in a Second Language?

Topic 6: How Do Attitude and Motivation Help in Learning a Second Language?

Topic 7: How Useful is Second Language Acquisition Research for Language Teaching?

Topic 8: What are the Goals of Language Teaching?

Introduction

Vivian Cook and David Singleton

Why should anybody be interested in how people acquire and use second languages? If you were brought up in a multilingual household or community, you probably take second languages for granted; acquiring a second language (L2) is no more interesting than acquiring a first is for monolinguals. Or, if you learnt a second language in school or at a college, you may have found it hard work and had continuing or even insurmountable problems; what would interest you is a quick fix that will allow you to learn the new language effortlessly and without pain. This book assumes that the acquisition and use of second languages is a normal part of human life, something that needs looking at scientifically because we know little about it and often depend upon folk wisdom for our views about it. Learning other languages is a crucial part of modern education and vital to people's lives in a world where it is increasingly difficult to get by on one language alone.

Since the 1960s the discipline called second language acquisition (SLA) research has investigated second languages, both in people who are accustomed to them by birth or situation and in those who are studying them in schools and colleges. The field started by concentrating on a few aspects of grammar but has widened to encompass the emotional life of L2 users, their gestures and their complex relationships with native speakers and with fellow L2 users, among many other topics: all human life may be involved with second languages, just as it is involved with the first language. SLA research now has journals, associations and conferences of its own in almost every country and has become so large that it has partly splintered into specialist groups of researchers concerned with particular aspects of the field such as pronunciation, multilingualism and generative grammar.

This book introduces readers to SLA research by exploring eight topics that have concerned people working in this field. Each topic provides an introductory discussion of the issues involved without presupposing any previous knowledge and it suggests where it may be followed up in more depth. The topics are treated independently rather than each building on the next, so that they can be read in any order that interests the reader. The two of us originally wrote four topics each and then edited each other's efforts. The final version preserves some of the stylistic differences between us to allow our personal voices to be heard. It is written partly interactively in that it asks readers to consider the issues based on their own experiences. The book is not then a comprehensive introduction to SLA research, of which there are many around, but a glimpse into how SLA researchers have tried to answer eight common questions about second language acquisition.

Doubtless there are innumerable topics that could be discussed about second language acquisition. How did we get it down to eight? First we considered the most common questions that people have asked us, like the best age for learning a language and how to learn second language vocabulary. Next we focused on the topics that we ourselves have researched over the years so that we could speak from research experience. Finally we wanted topics that are important for human beings everywhere, rather than explorations of theoretical or abstract issues. The final choice was then a combination of popularity, expertise and relevance.

So what *is* interesting about acquiring and using second languages? Here are some of the claims that are made in the eight topics:

- *A total of 43.5% of the residents of Toronto have a first language which is neither English nor French, the official languages of Canada.* This is one sign of the increasing multilingualism of the world even in countries that are officially bilingual like Canada. Probably across the globe L2 users outnumber those who speak only one language. Topic 1 'How Do Different Languages Connect in Our Minds?' is about the complicated relationship between the two languages in one mind.
- *Parents outperformed children going to live in the Netherlands in second language learning for the first five months of their stay.* The popular belief is that the younger you learn a language the better. But research shows this claim needs to be qualified in all sorts of ways, particularly in terms of the kinds of contact you have with people speaking the language. Topic 2 'Is There a Best Age for Learning a Second Language?' considers how age affects the outcome of second language learning, for better or for worse.
- *People speaking to foreigners use more high frequency vocabulary, less slang and fewer idioms.* The kind of language we hear has a crucial effect on our learning of vocabulary. We may encounter different forms of the language according to who is speaking and the situation we find ourselves in. Topic 3 'How Do People Acquire the Words of a Second Language?' reports how people go about learning the words of a second language, which is, for many learners, perceived as the most important part of second language acquisition.
- *Many early learners of a second language form basic sentences with two rules: they either put a verb after a noun or put a noun after a verb.* People construct second language grammar out of the language they hear and processes in their minds, often hitting on the same simple grammar, regardless of the first language they know or the second language they are acquiring. Topic 4 'How Important is Grammar in Acquiring and Using a Second Language?' is thus concerned with how people acquire the ability to put sentences together in the second language – grammar.
- *How you interpret before and after pictures in advertisements depends on the direction in which you learnt to read and write, either left-to-right or right-to-left.* The way in which you first learnt to read and write your first language affects not just the language you learn, but what you make of the world around you. Topic 5 'How Do People Learn to Write in a Second Language?' is about learning the mechanics of writing a second language, crucially important in these days of the internet.
- *The more you want to integrate with the community that uses the second language you are learning, the better you will learn the language.* Motivation is one of the keys to successful language acquisition, whether in the classroom or outside. Topic 6 'How Do Attitude and Motivation Help in Learning a Second Language?' describes the many competing views about how these personal aspects contribute to successful second language acquisition in the multilingual world of today.

- *The audiolingual language teaching method of dialogues and structure drills combined the psychological ideas of behaviourism with the linguistic ideas of American structuralism.* Language teaching is a product of the psychological and linguistic theories of its time, seldom connecting directly with SLA research. Topic 7 'How Useful is Second Language Acquisition Research for Language Teaching?' looks at how SLA research ideas can relate to language teaching methodologies, a vital matter for all teachers.
- *In London restaurants many non-Spanish speaking workers use Spanish as a lingua franca with other workers.* Second languages are practical forms of intercultural communication, most obviously in the global use of English as a lingua franca. Topic 8 'What are the Goals of Language Teaching?' discusses the diverse uses that people have for second languages and raises the fundamental question for education of *why* we should teach a second language.

We hope then that this book will lead the reader into the fascinating and important issues about second languages in people's minds and lives in the modern world, issues which have concerned us both all our working lives and which still continue to intrigue us.

1

How Do Different Languages Connect in Our Minds?

Vivian Cook

The underlying issue in second language acquisition (SLA) is how two or more languages connect to each other in the same mind. If we speak both English and Japanese, say, do we effectively keep them in separate English and Japanese compartments or are the languages mixed up together? This question is the raison d'être of SLA research and distinguishes it from first language acquisition research: when you have one language already in your mind, what happens when you acquire another?

What is a bilingual?

A starting point is the concept of bilingualism itself. This term means very contrary things to different people. Your answer to Question 2 in Box 1.1 gives away which of the meanings you subscribe to.

Starter: Being a bilingual   Box 1.1

(1)   Do you consider yourself a bilingual?
        Yes/No. Why/Why not?
(2)   Is a bilingual:
        (A)   a person who knows two languages equally well?
        (B)   a person who can use another language effectively?

A general definition of bilingualism might be that offered by Uriel Weinreich, a Yiddish-speaking American linguist, in 1953: 'The practice of alternately using two languages will be called bilingualism and the persons involved, bilinguals'.[1] But for most purposes this begs the question as it does not say how much, how often or how well the bilingual speaks the two languages. If I go into a restaurant in Florence and say *buona sera* does that make me a bilingual? If you can follow an Italian film without reading the subtitles are you a bilingual? In short, how much of a second language do you need to know to count as a bilingual?

Famous L2 users   Box 1.2

- Gandhi: Gujarati, English (+other Indian languages).
- Einstein: physicist: German, English.
- Picasso: artist: Spanish, French, Catalan.
- Marie Curie: physicist/chemist: Polish, French.
- Samuel Beckett: writer: English, French.
- Joseph Conrad: writer: Polish, French, English.
- Jorge Luis Borges: writer: Spanish, English.
- Martina Navratilova: tennis player: Czech, English.
- Erwin Schrödinger: physicist: English, German.
- Aung Sung Lee: politician: Burmese, English.
- Pope Francis: prelate: Spanish, Italian, German.

If you agreed with answer (A) that a bilingual is 'a person who knows two languages equally well', you are adopting the definition of American linguist Leonard Bloomfield, who said in the 1930s that bilingualism is 'native-like control of two languages'.[2] Probably the most common idea of bilingualism is that it means being able to speak two languages fluently in all circumstances. In this view, bilinguals can use both languages equally effectively and can readily pass for native speakers of either – balanced bilingualism in which neither language is dominant in the mind. This is sometimes called the 'maximal' definition of *bilingualism*: you couldn't have a higher target than perfection in both languages.

Such balanced bilinguals are hard to find. For one reason, bilinguals tend to use their two languages in different situations or speak them to different people rather than cover all occasions and all people with both languages. If you play tennis with a German-speaking partner and golf with a French-speaking partner, your use is likely to be skewed between the two languages. You may be good at writing essays in English but bad at writing them in your first language, or so Greek students in England have told me. It is hard to think of many people who use both languages equally for all of the possible ways they can use language. Balanced bilinguals in this sense are thin on the ground.

But there may be more maximal bilinguals around than one suspects. After all, if people are truly bilingual in this maximal sense, you won't be able to tell they are not native speakers in either language: they are invisible bilinguals. The film star Audrey Hepburn for example was bilingual from birth but one would never have known from her films; Prince Philip, the Queen's Consort, spoke English, German and French in childhood (and was christened Philippos). Presumably secret agents need this ability to survive undetected; certainly the Irish playwright Samuel Beckett successfully worked with the French Resistance in German-occupied France in World War Two.

If you agreed with answer (B) that a bilingual is 'a person who can use another language effectively', you are on the side of Einar Haugen, a Norwegian American, who claimed that bilingualism starts at 'the point where a speaker can first produce complete meaningful utterances in the other language'.[3] When an English speaker says *Bonjour* in a shop in France, they are using language bilingually: what they are saying is complete, meaningful and appropriate to the situation, even if totally predictable and banal. Bilingualism is a question of being able to use the second language in a meaningful way for certain things, not of being able to do everything.

Such a bilingual would have no chance at all of passing for a native speaker. They are nonetheless using the second language perfectly adequately for their own needs. I can get by as a visitor in restaurants and shops in Italy using hardly any Italian; if I lived there, I would doubtless need to expand my repertoire considerably. This is then the 'minimal' definition of *bilingual*; one couldn't imagine a lower target for learning a second language. Such bilinguals are extremely common around the world; indeed, on some counts, there are more people who use second languages in the world than there are pure monolinguals.

While we can all agree with Weinreich's definition of bilingualism as alternating between languages, the two opposing common meanings of the word *bilingual* are difficult to reconcile. The maximal definition is a virtually impossible counsel of perfection that can at best apply to a handful of people and tends to make people feel inferior who are in fact perfectly adequate second language users; they may be ashamed that their accent gives away that they are not native speakers even if this doesn't interfere with their communication. The maximal definition is thus too exclusive. The minimal definition on the other hand includes all the people in the world who have ever tried to communicate something in another language, which amounts to almost everybody. The minimal definition is then far too inclusive. The problem is you often don't know which of the senses of *bilingual* a particular person intends.

To avoid this dilemma, SLA researchers tend to employ the alternative term *L2 learner,* which has no overtones of either maximal or minimal bilingualism. But in my view *L2 learner* does have the implication that people who speak a second language will never finish learning it; you are condemned to be an L2 learner all your life apparently, never getting to the state of having learnt the language. Can someone who has been using a second language for decades like Swedish-speaking Björn Ulvaeus of Abba really still be called an L2 learner of English?

Hence I prefer the term *second language (L2) user* for 'somebody who is actively using a language other than their first'. This does not pin down a particular minimal or maximal use of the second language. *L2 user* is a convenient term for people who know more than one language without the overtones that cloud the words *bilingual* and *learner*. It involves making a distinction between using a language and learning a language; some people are indeed L2 learners in classrooms who do not use the other language for any real everyday purpose, say English children learning French; others interact each day of their lives with other people through more than one language, say the inhabitants of multilingual cities like Toronto, Berlin or New Delhi. Of course in some cases both learning and using are going on at the same time. A Polish worker coming to Ireland is doubtless both learning English and using it from the moment they arrive in Dublin, probably having been a school learner for many years. *L2 learner* in this book is complementary to *L2 user,* one concerned with the process of acquiring another language, the other with the process of using it. This does not, however, mean that we can totally avoid the term *bilingual*, partly because it is used in so much of the research. Nevertheless we will try to draw a line between *L2 users* and *L2 learners* wherever possible, even if many people are effectively both, like the Polish worker.

Characteristics of L2 users

So what are L2 users actually like? In one way the question is as meaningless as asking what human beings are like. L2 users come in as many shapes and sizes as monolinguals. Any generalisation is going to have to cover the whole gamut of human beings.

There are certainly a great many L2 users about. The figures in Box 1.3 give some idea of their numbers. The authoritative online reference source for information about languages is *Ethnologue*.[4] To calculate how multilingual a country is, they use a statistic called the linguistic diversity index (LDI) invented by Joseph Greenberg.[5] The LDI represents the odds of meeting someone in your country who speaks a different language from you. In Papua New Guinea, where 830 languages are spoken, you have a likelihood of 99 in 100 that a random stranger will speak another language; in Cuba, where four languages are spoken, there is only a one in 1000 chance. In between is China (296 languages) with a 51 in 100 chance and Japan (16 languages) with a three in 100 chance.

Some facts and figures

Box 1.3

- **90%**: proportion of children in Europe learning English as a second language.
- **56%**: proportion of EU citizens who can converse in two languages.
- **42.6%**: proportion of speakers of other languages than English in California.
- **43.5%**: proportion of people in Toronto whose first language is neither English nor French.
- **4.2 million**: number of people in the UK in 2011 whose first language is not English.
- **546,000**: number of Polish speakers in the UK.
- **46.5%**: proportion of Presidents of the USA who spoke more than one language.

If you assume that more languages means more L2 users, this gives some measure of how multilingual a country is: Papua New Guinea should have very many L2 users, Cuba rather fewer. The LDI is, however, based on the proportion of monolinguals of different languages in a country and makes no claims about their use of a second language. So it cannot easily be applied to countries which have several languages that are spoken in different areas, since the speakers may not actually mix with each other. For example, Switzerland has an LDI of 55 in 100 but the French, German, Romansch and Italian speakers live in geographically different segments of the country. Similarly Canada has an LDI of 55 out of 100, despite the two official languages, French and English, being in separate provinces (with the exception of bilingual New Brunswick). Nevertheless this does suggest that the majority of people in the world probably use more than one language successfully in their everyday lives, even if they are far from maximal bilinguals.

People who speak only one language tend to assume that bilingualism is a problem. Yet there is no more a problem of bilingualism than there is a problem of monolingualism. L2 users don't have any more mental or social problems, or educational difficulties than anybody else. Claims to the contrary are usually based, not so much on their bilingualism per se – a phenomenon involving language – as on the emotional, social and economic plights of immigrants or minority groups – largely social and economic deprivation.

Parents often worry about whether it is a good idea to bring up their children bilingually. There is no evidence that bilingualism itself harms a child; many argue that it brings unique advantages to the child in their ability to use language, to reason and to understand other people, as we will see later. For example Canadian children in bilingual schools were better able to communicate an idea to a blindfolded person than monolingual children[6]; they were more sensitive to people's communication needs. In England the advice used to be to avoid using two languages with Down's Syndrome children as it confused them; yet an Indian visitor told me how her Down's Syndrome child naturally speaks the four languages that surround him.

What are L2 users like?

So what are the characteristics of this diverse group of L2 users? Let us look at them as people in their own right, not just as people who are poor imitations of native speakers. Here are some of the ways in which L2 users are unique.

L2 users think differently

When you learn another language, you start to think in slightly different ways. A traditional reason for teaching children another language was that it trained their brains. In England it was Latin that was supposed to do the trick. Boris Johnson, the current Mayor of London, has pronounced 'Latin and Greek are great intellectual disciplines, forcing young minds to think in a logical and analytical way'. But all learning of another language probably changes people's thinking to some extent, not just classical languages; L2 users no longer see the world in quite the same way as monolinguals. As the Italian film director Federico Fellini is supposed to have said, 'A different language is a different vision of life'.

For example, speakers of English have a single colour which they call *blue*, whether it's the blue of the sky or the blue of a sapphire. Speakers of some other languages see two colours, corresponding to English *light blue* and *dark blue*, called *ble* and *ghalazio* in Greek, *azzurro* and *blu* in Italian and *sinij* and *goluboj* in Russian. Where an English eye sees one colour, speakers of other languages see two. The way you perceive colours goes with your language. Just compare a street scene in Tokyo with one in Kuala Lumpur or one in Oslo to appreciate people's different ideas of colour.

Learning another language, however, brings the two colour systems into conflict; will you change your perception of colour to fit the new language or will you perceive the same colours when you speak the new language? When Greeks learn English, they have to collapse two colours into one and this affects the way they see colours, not just their words for the colours.[7] Their first language meanings for *ble* and *ghalazio* are subtly different from those of monolingual Greeks, as they are for Russian and Japanese speakers who know other languages. Learning another language infiltrates many areas of your mind, not just those devoted to language.

Some researchers have investigated the changes in thinking in L2 users through the stories that bilinguals tell of their lives. Take an important concept like 'friend'; do you change your idea of friendship when you have to take part in another culture or do you stick to the same idea? Mary Besemeres looked at a range of these bilingual histories and found the information displayed in Box 1.4.[8]

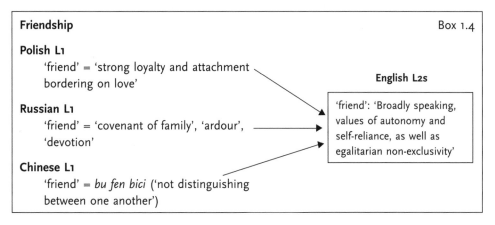

Friendship Box 1.4

Polish L1
'friend' = 'strong loyalty and attachment bordering on love'

Russian L1
'friend' = 'covenant of family', 'ardour', 'devotion'

Chinese L1
'friend' = *bu fen bici* ('not distinguishing between one another')

English L2s
'friend': 'Broadly speaking, values of autonomy and self-reliance, as well as egalitarian non-exclusivity'

The English concept of 'friend' reflects 'values of autonomy and self-reliance, as well as egalitarian non-exclusivity'. To a Pole however the concept conveys 'strong loyalty and attachment bordering on love'. A Polish person learning to live in an English-speaking society has therefore to tone down the strength of meaning of 'friendship'. The Russian concept similarly has stronger overtones – a 'covenant of family' – than English. To a Chinese person a friend is so close you do not need to distinguish him or her from yourself; you wouldn't thank yourself for something so you don't need to thank a friend. In most of these languages the casual English use of the word *friend* for Facebook contacts would be unthinkable. Complex changes in thinking are necessary to function effectively in another society. A young Polish girl in Canada was asked by another girl if she would be her friend and she replied that she didn't know her well enough yet[9]: the two concepts of friendship had collided and the Canadian girl was upset at the apparent rejection.

L2 users have a better feel for language

One of the obvious changes in people who know more than two languages is a better feel for language in general. One sign is the number of bilingual writers: Vladimir Nabokov wrote *Lolita* in Russian and then did his own version in English; Samuel Beckett first wrote *Waiting for Godot* in French. André Brink, the South African novelist, writes his novels switching between English and Afrikaans when he feels like it; after he has finished, he decides which language should be used for publication. Seventeenth century English poets like Milton and Dryden often wrote in Latin; Milton was made 'Secretary for Foreign Tongues' for the Cromwell government: Dryden earned a living as a translator for some years. Artistic creativity with language often goes with bilingualism.

A crucial element in human language is the arbitrary link between the meaning of words and their actual sounds or spellings. A rose by any other name would indeed smell as sweet. But it is very difficult for many of us to break the shackles of our first language. Can a speaker of English really accept that a *méiguì* (Chinese for 'rose') or a *triantafyllo* (Greek for 'rose') smells as sweet as a *rose*? One of the advantages of being an L2 user is that we become more aware of the sheer arbitrariness of language. For example young children believe that long words go with big objects, short words with small ones, a *hippopotamus* must be much bigger than an *ant*. Bilingual children are however better than monolinguals at seeing that this does not work: a small word like *train* may refer to a large thing while a long word like *caterpillar* may refer to something quite small.[10] Knowing another language helps bilingual children to realise that size of word has nothing to do with size of object.

Bilingual children are also far better at a task in which they are told that *spaghetti* is a new word for *bird* and asked to say what *Birds fly* would be.[11] *Spaghettis fly* comes to their minds much more readily than to their monolingual peers. Knowing another language means you appreciate better that anything could be called by any name: names are arbitrary. In a sense bilingual children believe a rose by any other name would smell as sweet while monolinguals are unconvinced.

L2 users speak their first language slightly differently

L2 users also have a slightly different knowledge of their first language from monolinguals. While many languages have a pair of phonemes /p/ and /b/ as in *pier/beer*, the actual sounds vary slightly according to when voicing from the vocal cords starts after the consonant, called Voice Onset Time (VOT). If you speak two languages that differ in VOT, say English *beer/pier* versus French *bière/pierre*, you have to use slightly different timings for the /p~b/ sounds in each language. Or do you? Some L2 users adopt an in-between timing for speaking *both* languages that is not the same as either their L1 or their L2.[12] Their pronunciation of their first language is then marginally different from that of monolinguals.

The same is true of the processing of grammar in the first language. For example French speakers who know English react against French sentences using the perfectly acceptable middle voice *Un tricot de laine se lave à l'eau froide.* (*A wool sweater washes in cold water) compared to those who don't know English.[13] Child L1 speakers of English learning Cherokee as a heritage language in the USA tend to over-regularise past tense forms such as *taked* in English more than their monolingual contemporaries (though other areas showed no differences).[14]

A second language also makes a difference to your emotional life. An L2 user is bound to have different emotions from a monolingual. Your personality and your identity feel different in another language.

Something of the complex effects of language on the emotional life of L2 users emerged from a piece of research by Jean-Marc Dewaele in which 1459 people who spoke more than one language – 459 actually spoke five – answered the questions 'Does the phrase "I love you" have the same emotional weight for you in your different languages? Which language does it feel strongest in?'[15] Language and emotions are closely intertwined; saying *I love you* evokes different feelings according to the language you're speaking. The results are given in Boxes 1.5 and 1.6. For 45 out of 100 the first language was strongest; 25 out of 100 thought another language; 30 out of 100 thought both. The same kind of declaration of love may then have a different force in the different languages the person speaks.

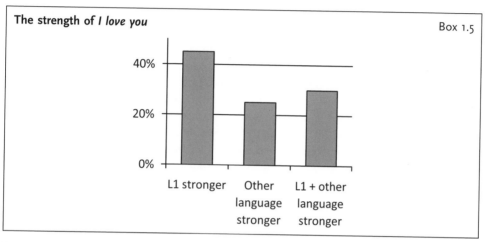

The strength of *I love you*   Box 1.5

Two L2 users' views of 'I love you'   Box 1.6

I feel the strongest force of this phrase in English. This phrase sounds romantic and passionate. In Japanese it sounds awkward. It simply means 'let's register for our marriage'. Too factual and not emotional at all. Young lovers in Hong Kong seldom say this phrase in Cantonese. They say it in English instead. Perhaps Cantonese isn't a romantic language at all. Personally I feel the strongest emotional force saying it in English particularly.
   Maggie (Chinese L1, English L2, Japanese L3)
I think it has more emotional weight for me in English than in Spanish. I feel more comfortable saying it in Spanish than in English.
   Darragh (English L1, French L2, Spanish L3, Irish L4)

A knowledge of more than one language enables L2 users to do things that monolinguals cannot. One is that, rather than using one language at a time in 'monolingual' mode, as François Grosjean terms it, they can effectively use both at once in 'bilingual' mode.[16] Most of the time their choice of mode may be invisible. Language teachers who ban the students' first language from the classroom might be shattered to know how much it is being used in the privacy of the students' minds.

The visible sign of this ability to use two languages at once is codeswitching – alternating between two languages within the same situation or conversation. Here is a Malaysian teacher talking in the staffroom: *Jadi I tanya, how can you say that when ... geram betul I* ('So I asked how can you say that when ... I was so mad'). A German train proclaims on its side *Eurostrand macht happy* ('Eurostrand makes you happy'). Some shop names depend upon the customer knowing another language, say the bilingual pun in the

English wine-merchants *The Cellar d'Or* (i.e. French *d'or* 'golden' versus English *door*) or the language switch between article and noun in *The Garaje* (a fast-food outlet in Spanish-speaking Valparaiso).

Codeswitching is a part of most L2 users' everyday lives when they talk to other people who share the same language. Box 1.7 gives a longer example of a gossip column in a Gibraltar online newspaper *Panorama* that codeswitches between Spanish and English.[17] Research has revealed complicated rules for when you can switch language, based on what you are talking about – Spanish speakers think English is more suitable for talking about money – and on the role of the person you are talking to – serving your sister in your shop means switching to a second language to show she is not getting special privileges. Codeswitching is a complex use of language that draws on two or more grammars and two or more sets of vocabulary virtually instantaneously. It's not just that someone knows a number of grammars, mental lexicons and pronunciation systems, but that they can effortlessly switch from one to the other in a moment. Every aspect of the L2 users' languages must be closely bound together for this to happen.

Corriendo in the colours of Spain   Box 1.7

Bueno hija, el new Governator is going to Brussels to see al quien entrego Hong Kong to the Chinese, que te parece?

Simply que cuando venga to our Gibraltar este James Bond and I see him in Main Street le voy a decir que he needs our permission, my dear.

Claro, pero ten cuidao porque he has been un tipo Bond y ese sabe hasta los colores de los calzoncillos de tu husband.

My dear, that is no secret. They are red, white and blue – and very proud of it.

At least he is not like the outgoing Governator, El Duro, who went jogging dressed in the colours of Spain – what a pain!

Currently the most well-known model of codeswitching is the 4M model proposed by Carol Myers-Scotton.[18] The 4 Ms stand for four types of morphemes – the smallest meaningful grammatical unit. The idea is that codeswitching uses the overall grammatical structure from one language, the 'matrix' language, and slots morphemes from the other language, the 'embedded language', into this structure. So the sentence:

> *Bueno hija, el new Governator is going to Brussels to see al quien entrego Hong Kong to the Chinese, que te parece?*

consists of an English matrix:

> *... new ... is going to Brussels to see ... Hong Kong to the Chinese...?*

into which certain Spanish words and phrases are embedded:

> *Bueno hija, el ... Governator ... al quien entrego ... , que te parece?*

To the monolingual, codeswitching has often appeared a careless slip-shod manner of speaking, adopted either because the speakers don't know enough words in the second language or because they want to hide what they are saying from other people. Weinreich indeed called it a deviant behaviour pattern.[1] Parents have often been perturbed when their bilingual children codeswitch, thinking they are just mixing up languages. But codeswitching is, on the one hand, a normal part of the L2 user's language repertoire with a complex system of rules for its use, on the other an amazing feat of tightrope walking in which L2 users constantly balance the two languages in terms of grammar, vocabulary and pronunciation. Even very young children are not mixing languages at random but according to the rules of codeswitching.[19] Codeswitching is effectively a skill unique to L2 users that monolinguals can't match. The only monolinguals who do anything similar are those who can switch between dialects of the same language. But this seems confined to a very few, such as Gillian Anderson of *X-Files* fame, who can effortlessly switch between British and American dialects.

Summary: L2 users often: Box 1.8

- think differently;
- have a better feel for language;
- have slightly different knowledge of their first languages;
- feel different emotions;
- can use bilingual modes of language.

Overall, most of these characteristics of L2 users are undoubtedly advantages rather than disadvantages. English/Chinese L2 users are better at understanding geometric ideas than their monolingual peers.[20] Hungarian children who are learning English write better essays in Hungarian.[21] L2 users even tend to get Alzheimer's five years later on average than monolinguals.[22] The only mental handicap that L2 users suffer seems to be slightly slower reaction times to some words, presumably due to the enlarged nature of the L2 user's language system.[23]

Two languages in one mind

So how do the two languages relate in one mind? Back in the 1950s, Uriel Weinreich proposed that there were three kinds of bilinguals.[1] His famous example is how the meaning of the first and second language words for 'book' can link in bilingual minds. Let us take the English word *book* and the French word *livre*, both of which connect to the concept of 'book' 📖 (though, as we have seen, the concept itself may vary between languages, say 📖 and ▢). The names he used for the three types have been slightly changed by later researchers; we will stick to the modern labels.

Some L2 users of English and French keep the two languages well apart. They know what *book* means and they know what *livre* means but they don't make a connection between them. While they can use both languages, in effect they can't translate between them. These are called 'coordinate' bilinguals, shown in Figure 1.1.

📖 ←————→ *book* (English L1)

□ ←————→ *livre* (French L2)

Figure 1.1 *Coordinate bilinguals*

This type corresponds to the view common in language teaching that the first language only gets in the way of L2 learning; when you come in to the second language classroom, you should park your first language at the door. From the Direct Method of the 19th century right down to the task-based learning of the 21st, language teaching has prioritised coordinate bilinguals.

Other L2 users have a single concept of 📖 that links to the two words in the different languages, *book* and *livre*. In this case the two languages are related to each other through a shared concept. They are called 'compound bilinguals', seen in Figure 1.2.

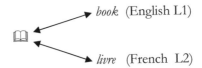

Figure 1.2 *Compound bilinguals*

No current mainstream teaching method seems to rely on this type of L2 user, though some 'fringe' methods have encouraged it, for example Dodson's Bilingual Method[24] in which L2 sentences are given meaning through the L1, and Concurrent Language Teaching in which the teacher switches from one language to the other according to pre-set rules.[25]

A third kind of L2 user links the L2 word *livre* to the L1 word *book* rather than directly to the concept. So they know what French *livre* means by linking it to the English *book* which eventually leads them to the meaning 📖. Their second language ties in to their first language via translation equivalents. These are called 'subordinate' bilinguals, as seen in Figure 1.3.

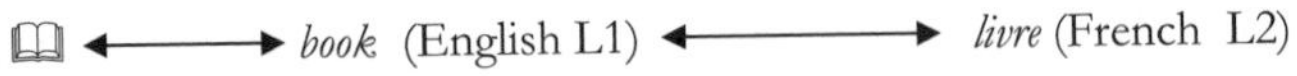

📖 ←————→ *book* (English L1) ←————→ *livre* (French L2)

Figure 1.3 *Subordinate bilinguals*

Many researchers have now reduced the three types to coordinate and compound, considering subordinate bilingualism to be a form of coordinate bilingualism. Nevertheless subordinate bilingualism corresponds to language teaching methods that use translation for teaching, the basis for the teaching of Latin and French in England for many years and the way that modern languages are still frequently taught at universities. I was taught French by a method which involved learning lists of vocabulary such as *le jubé: roodloft* – not that I found out what a roodloft was in English for many years.

Summary: Weinreich's kinds of bilinguals   Box 1.9

- *coordinate bilinguals* keep the languages separate;
- *compound bilinguals* combine the two languages together;
- *subordinate bilinguals* link the second language to the first.

More recently the relationship between the languages has been visualised in terms of an integration continuum, as shown in Figure 1.4.[26]

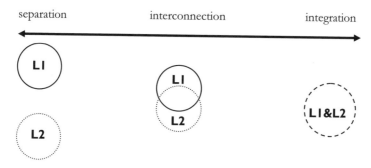

Figure 1.4   *The integration continuum of relationships between two languages in one mind*

The two languages in the L2 user's mind go from total separation at one pole to total integration at the other. So at one end come coordinate bilinguals who keep the languages quite separate, at the other end compound bilinguals who have completely merged them. Doubtless nobody could keep both languages totally separate and nobody is completely incapable of telling them apart. Nevertheless, total separation and total integration are the ideal forms; L2 users are all placed somewhere in between along the integration continuum. Expressing the relationship between the languages as a gradual continuum rather than an either/or choice means individuals are spread out over a range rather than squeezed into two or three categories like Weinreich's.

This does not imply that people progress from any one end of the continuum to the other – the continuum doesn't have a single direction. A person may succeed in integrating the languages more over time or in separating them more, say someone taught by a teaching method that emphasises separation who learns to codeswitch in a multilingual situation or a child brought up in a bilingual home who learns to keep the languages apart at school.

But the integration continuum also applies to particular aspects of language use. An individual's speaking skill can be more integrated than their writing skill, say. Or the vocabulary of their first and second languages might be integrated in one vast store while their two pronunciation systems stay quite separate. Integration applies not just to the relationship of the two languages as wholes but also to their different elements.

Many people indeed think of the first and second language vocabulary as forming a single whole. If you show L2 users pictures of objects and name them in one of their languages, their eyes are attracted by objects that have similar names in the other language: they never switch off either language entirely.[27] A classic study demonstrated that, when presented with the word *coin*, L2 users of English and French activated both the French meaning 'corner' and the English meaning 'piece of money' whichever language they were using.[28] On the other hand the word associations of L2 users are unlike those of monolinguals of either language.[29] When you learn another language, the result may not be the merger of two languages but something new – if you merge hydrogen and oxygen you get water. If you merge a first language and a second, you get something new, which is identical to neither the first nor the second language.

In terms of thinking, integration means merging the two concepts into one in the mind; rather than having two blues, the L2 user would have a single colour, possibly not the same as the monolingual's. Separation would mean the two concepts being kept distinct; the L2 user would switch from having two blues to having one according to whether they were speaking English or Greek.

The integration continuum thus recognises many possible relationships between the languages in someone's mind. Human beings do not shed their diversity when they become L2 users. The range of language knowledge and use is even wider in L2 users than in monolinguals.

Postscript   Box 1.10

Has your view of bilinguals changed after reading this chapter?
- Do you now think there are more bilinguals in the world than you thought?
- Would you change your answer to Box 1.1 Question 2?
- Would you be more or less cautious about saying *I love you* in a second language?
- Have you spotted any effects of your second language on your first?
- How do you think the languages you know are related in your mind?

Further reading

Some books that deal with these issues at greater length in a similar way are:

Cook, V.J. (2008) *Second Language Learning and Language Teaching*, 4th edition. London: Hodder Education.

Grosjean, F. (2010) *Bilingual: Life and Reality*. Boston, MA: Harvard U.P.

Ortega, L. (2009) *Understanding Second Language Acquisition*. London: Hodder Education.

Rich, K. (2010) *Dreaming in Hindi: Life in Translation*. London: Portobello Books.

References

1.   Weinreich, U. (1953) *Languages in Contact.* The Hague: Mouton.

2.   Bloomfield, L. (1933) *Language.* New York: Holt Rinehart Winston.

3.   Haugen, E. (1953) *The Norwegian Language in America.* Philadelphia: University of Pennsylvania Press.

4.   Lewis, M.P., Simons, G.F. and Fennig, C.D. (eds) (2013) *Ethnologue: Languages of the World,* 17th edition. Dallas, Texas: SIL International. Online at: http://www.ethnologue.com.

5.   Greenberg, J.H. (1956) The measurement of linguistic diversity. *Language* 32 (1), 109–115.

6.   Genesee, F., Tucker, R. and Lambert, W.E. (1975) Communication skills of bilingual children. *Child Development* 46, 1010–1014.

7.   Athanasopoulos, P. (2009) Cognitive representation of colour in bilinguals: The case of Greek blues. *Bilingualism: Language and Cognition* 12, 83–95.

8.   Besemeres, M. (2011) Personal narratives by bilinguals as a form of inquiry into bilingualism. In V.J. Cook and B. Bassetti (eds) *Language and Bilingual Cognition.* New York: Psychology Press, 479–506.

9.   Hoffman, E. (1989) *Lost in Translation: A Life in a New Language.* London: Minerva.

10. Bialystok, E. (1991) Metalinguistic dimensions of bilingual language proficiency. In E. Bialystok (ed.) *Language Processing in Bilingual Children.* Cambridge: Cambridge University Press, 113–140.

11. Ben-Zeev, S. (1977) The influence of bilingualism on cognitive strategy and cognitive development. *Child Development* 48, 1009–1018.

12. Wrembel, M. (2011) Cross-linguistic influence in third language acquisition of Voice Onset Time. *ICPhS* XVII, 2157–2160.

13. Balcom, P. (2003) Cross-linguistic influence of L2 English on middle constructions in L1 French. In V.J. Cook (ed.) *L2 Effects on the L1.* Clevedon: Multilingual Matters, 168–192.

14. Hirata-Edds, T. (2011) Influence of second language Cherokee immersion on children's development of past tense in their first language, English. *Language Learning* 61 (3), 700–733.

15. Dewaele, J-M. (2008) The emotional weight of 'I love you' in multilinguals' languages. *Journal of Pragmatics* 40 (10), 1753–1780.

16. Grosjean, F. (1998) Studying bilinguals: Methodological and conceptual issues. *Bilingualism: Language and Cognition* 1 (2), 131–149.

17. *Panorama* (no date) Online at: http://www.panorama.gi/. Accessed 15/01/2014.

18. Myers-Scotton, C. (2006) *Multiple Voices: An Introduction to Bilingualism.* Oxford: Wiley-Blackwell.

19. Genesee, F. (2003) Portrait of the bilingual child. In V. Cook (ed.) *Portraits of the L2 User.* Clevedon: Multilingual Matters, 161–179.

20. Han, A.Y. and Ginsburg, H.P. (2001) Chinese and English mathematics language: The relation between linguistic clarity and mathematics performance. *Mathematical Thinking and Learning* 3, 201–220.

21. Kecskes, I. and Papp, T. (2000) *Foreign Language and Mother Tongue*. Hillsdale, NJ: Lawrence Erlbaum.

22. Bialystok, E., Craik, F.I.M. and Freedman, M. (2007) Bilingualism as a protection against the onset of symptoms of dementia. *Neuropsychologia* 45, 459–464.

23. Magiste, E. (1986) Selected issues in second and third language learning. In J. Vaid (ed.) *Language Processing in Bilinguals: Psycholinguistic and Neurolinguistic Perspectives*. Hillsdale, NJ: Lawrence Erlbaum, 97–122.

24. Dodson, C.J. (1967) *Language Teaching and The Bilingual Method*. London: Pitman.

25. Faltis, C.J. (1989) Codeswitching and bilingual schooling: An examination of Jacobson's new concurrent approach. *Journal of Multilingual and Multicultural Development* 10 (2), 117–127.

26. Cook, V.J. (2003) Introduction: The changing L1 in the L2 user's mind. In V.J. Cook (ed.) *Effects of the Second Language on the First*. Clevedon: Multilingual Matters, 1–18.

27. Spivey, M.J. and Marian, V. (1999) Cross talk between native and second languages: Partial activation of an irrelevant lexicon. *Psychological Science* 10, 181–184.

28. Beauvillain, C. and Grainger, J. (1987) Accessing interlexical homographs: Some limitations of a language-selective access. *Journal of Memory and Language* 26, 658–672.

29. Zareva, A. (2010) Multicompetence and L2 users' associative links: Being unlike nativelike. *International Journal of Applied Linguistics* 20 (1), 2–22.

2

Is There a Best Age for Learning a Second Language?

David Singleton

Starter					Box 2.1

Tick the best age to start each of these activities:

- using a computer   ☐ under 10   ☐ 10–20   ☐ 21–35   ☐ 36–60   ☐ over 60
- falling in love   ☐ under 10   ☐ 10–20   ☐ 21–35   ☐ 36–60   ☐ over 60
- learning to sing   ☐ under 10   ☐ 10–20   ☐ 21–35   ☐ 36–60   ☐ over 60
- driving a car   ☐ under 10   ☐ 10–20   ☐ 21–35   ☐ 36–60   ☐ over 60
- learning another language   ☐ under 10   ☐ 10–20   ☐ 21–35   ☐ 36–60   ☐ over 60

The word on the street: Popular beliefs on age and second language learning

According to most people's view of things, the answer to the question posed in the title 'Is There a Best Age for Learning a Second Language?' is 'Of course'; the age factor is crucial to second language learning. The general view is that childhood is obviously the best time to start to learn a second language. This is not a surprising reaction. After all, first language development is something that happens in childhood and so the general assumption is that children are better equipped to acquire languages than adolescents and adults. Moreover, common experience tells us that starting to learn *anything* early in life – the violin, chess, golf – often seems to yield dramatic advantages.

Our observations of differences between children and adults trying to get to grips with a new language often tend to reinforce our notion that when it comes to learning additional languages, younger = better. How often do we see young immigrant children with a perfectly functional command of the language of the host country acting as interpreters for their parents and grandparents? The British psychologist J.S. Tomb commented in 1925 on a similar phenomenon observable in English families in India in the days of the Raj[1]:

> It is a common experience in the district of Bengal in which the author resides to hear English children 3 or 4 years old ... conversing freely at different times with their parents in English, with their *ayahs* (nurses) in Bengali, with the garden coolies in Santali, and with the house-servants in Hindustani, while their parents have learnt with the aid of a *munshi* (teacher) and much laborious effort just sufficient Hindustani to comprehend what the house-servants are saying ... and to issue simple orders to them ...

Starting ages of some champion golfers	Box 2.2
Arnold Palmer	4 years
Jack Nicklaus	10 years
Seve Ballesteros	7 years
Tiger Woods	3 years
Rory McIlroy	18 months

Interestingly, the children referred to had vastly more contact with the Indian house-staff than their parents. So it is generally with children who come to reside in a country or a region where the dominant language is different from their home language, who tend to become more quickly and more deeply embedded in their host community than their parents. This is not to deny the reality of an age factor; we know that our capacities begin to decline from quite an early age. It is important, however, to recognize that a range of age-*related* factors as well as purely maturational factors need to be taken into account.

We shall return later to the effects of being instructed in a second language early in life, but it is probably worth briefly noting at this stage that such effects are by no means consistently positive. In some countries commercial companies advertise English language services aimed at very young children (between two and four years), the suggestion being that early learning of this important international language will give the children in question a clear advantage in their later educational and professional careers. The researcher Joanna Rokita decided to investigate the claims of one such company,[2] and was fairly scathing about what she found. Her conclusion, basically, was that the achievements of the young instructed L2 learners she studied were deeply unimpressive, their command of English consisting largely in the parroting of formulas and very rarely having anything resembling a spontaneous, communicative dimension.

Ola's experience of English in her own words   Box 2.3

My name is Ola. I'm Polish. I was introduced to English for the first time at school at the age of 18. Until that time my only foreign language had been Russian. I made two brief visits to English-speaking countries in my twenties, and then, at the age of 28, I moved to Dublin, where I have now been living for seven years. My English is by no means perfect but quite a lot of English-speakers I talk to think I'm Irish.

(Name changed)

It is also worth saying that attempting to learn a second language in adulthood, even mature adulthood, even old age, is certainly not bound to be a dismal failure. Whenever I hear someone say 'At my time of life I'm too old to be learning other languages', my response is always the same – namely, that in this matter, as in so many others, age is no excuse! People with long experience of teaching additional languages to older adults are very clear that such students positively excel in some domains. For example, many years ago the adult educator Max Brändle said of older adult learners of foreign languages that 'in the case of reading skills they invariably set the highest learning goals' and that they seem to have 'little difficulty with grammatical principles and storing lexical items'.[3] Brändle conceded that older adults sometimes have problems with 'auditory imitation and memorizing' as well as with 'oral response' but he certainly did not represent these as insuperable obstacles to progress.

As for younger adults, they can reach very high levels indeed of second language proficiency. A dramatic illustration of this is provided by the case of the late Robert Maxwell, whose life was in many ways remarkable but ended tragically in 1991 amidst a financial scandal. Maxwell was a member of the UK House of Commons, owner of a number of British newspapers and publishing houses, and Chairman of Oxford United Football Club – making frequent appearances on British radio and television. In my younger years, I assumed, like many other Britons, that he was British born and bred, and certainly a native speaker of the English language. In fact, Robert Maxwell started life as Ján Ludvík Hoch in a Yiddish-speaking Jewish family in pre-Second World War Czechoslovakia. His first significant encounter with English was in 1940, when, at the age of 17, he arrived in Britain escaping from the Nazis. Many of us know people whose L2 learning histories and L2 attainments are similar to Robert Maxwell's. The chances are, though, that unless they actually reveal the facts about their non-English-speaking past to us, we simply assume that English is their first language.

In sum, then, while there are good reasons for supposing that learning an additional language in childhood may tend to yield better results than starting later, and, while there seems to be evidence in favour of this view from our observation of immigrants, the truth of this matter is certainly not simple. Learning additional languages at an early age in a formal instructional setting, for example, does not always bring about the brilliant results people sometimes hope for or expect. On the other hand, learning a second or third language in the adult years – even old age – can sometimes lead to very solid results, and, in the case of younger adults, to nativelike performance.

Summary   Box 2.4

- The question of age is connected with how much learners talk to people who speak the second language, often easier for children in immigrant/expat situations.
- Many people who start learning as adults in fact acquire a second language to a high level.
- Teaching a second language to young children is often unsuccessful.

Views on age   Box 2.5

(1) How many people have you actually met who were invisible bilinguals who started the second language after 15, like Robert Maxwell?

    o   1–5   6–10   more than 10

(2) How many people have you actually met who are highly competent, though clearly not native speakers, who started the second language after 15?

    o   1–5   6–10   more than 10

(3) Does your experience then support the popular belief in the advantages of learning other languages in early childhood?

The experience of immigrants:
The research background

The case of immigrant users of the languages of their host countries has already featured in the introductory discussion above, and we have noted that the best evidence for age-related advantages in L2 learning appears to come by comparing younger and older immigrants. Let us now take a closer look at the experience and second language attainment of immigrants.

From the middle of the last century down to the present day, there has been a steady stream of research investigating the idea that younger arrivals in a country where the dominant language is different from the immigrants' home language are more likely than older arrivals to end up passing for native speakers of the new language. Some of the studies in question are listed in Box 2.6, and, in all the cases featuring in this particular list, the findings support the notion of younger = better.

Classic research on the age factor   Box 2.6

Asher & Garcia (1969): better pronunciation of English tended to be associated with immigrants who had arrived in the USA between one and five years of age rather than with those who had arrived at later ages.[4]

Seliger et al. (1975): most people who had immigrated under the age of nine reported passing for native speakers of the host country language; most who had arrived after the age of 16 felt they had a foreign accent.[5]

Patkowski (1980): the grammatical competence in English of immigrants arriving in the USA before the age of 15 was better on average than that of those who had arrived at later ages.[6]

Hyltenstam (1992): immigrants to Sweden who had arrived after the age of seven produced more lexical and grammatical errors in Swedish than those who had arrived before the age of six.[7]

Piske et al. (2002): Italian immigrants to Canada who had arrived as children tended to have less of a foreign accent in English than those who had arrived as adolescents or adults.[8]

To be noted is that all the studies showing a general second language advantage for immigrants arriving as children over later arrivals involve participants who have been in the new country for a considerable period – five years or more. The advantage in question seems to require a certain period of time to manifest itself. For example, a famous study by Catherine Snow and Marianne Hoefnagel-Höhle of English-speaking migrants to the Netherlands of various ages found that, after the first four or five months of residence in the Netherlands, the proficiency in the newly acquired Dutch of the adolescents and adults was markedly superior to that of the children in all areas except pronunciation, but that the older participants' advantage began to be noticeably eroded in the following months.[9]

Also worth attending to is the fact that in the immigrant studies the younger = better tendency is just that – a tendency. It is not the case that *all* immigrants who arrive in their new country in childhood end up with a perfect command of the language of the host country; nor is it the case that those who arrive later in life systematically fail to attain the levels reached by younger arrivals.

Moreover the emphasis in most of the studies of immigrants coping with a new language has been very firmly on proficiency attainment in the second language in question. Much less investigative energy has been devoted to what happens to the immigrants' first language while they are coming to grips with the language of their host country. In particular this relates to language dominance – which language is the stronger in the user's mind. One claim is that immigrants that arrive before the age of 10 are quite likely to switch their dominant language from their home language to the language of the host community, whereas those arriving after the age of 10 are likely to maintain the dominance of the home language.[10]

The nature of the immigrant's relationship with the new language cannot be explained simply in terms of maturation, although it clearly has an age dimension. Box 2.7 sets out some differences in the experience of younger and older immigrants in terms of what they arrive with and in terms of aspects of their life in the new country, which can plausibly be seen as impinging on proficiency attainment in the host country language and on the role of this language among immigrants arriving at different ages.

Typical profiles in terms of self-identification on arrival and experiences in the new country (drawing on Bialystok, 1997[11] and Jia & Aaronson, 1999[10]) Box 2.7	
Age of immigration	Typical profile
Age 6	Linguistico-cultural identity not yet fully formed.
	Frequent contact at school with children from outside their own linguistico-cultural community; possibility of friendships with such children little influenced by linguistico-cultural affiliation.
	Schooling through host community language, involving specifically linguistic instruction in relation to literacy.
Age 12	Linguistico-cultural identity well on the way to being fully formed.
	Frequent contact at school with children from outside their own linguistic community; considerable degree of choice regarding friendships – probably influenced by linguistico-cultural affiliation.
	Schooling through host community language, usually not involving specifically linguistic instruction unless a language support teacher is made available.
Age 24	Linguistico-cultural identity fully formed.
	Contact with people outside own linguistic community dependent on nature of job (in some cases most colleagues may be from their own community); friendships entirely a matter of choice and typically influenced by linguistico-cultural affiliation.
	No schooling through or in relation to host community language unless evening/weekend classes are opted for.

In particular these relate to the concept of linguistico-cultural identity. As children grow so do they begin to identify with a particular language or cultural identity. In multilingual nurseries children seem not to be aware that the children come from different backgrounds. They gradually become aware of this as they mature and the kinds of relationships they have change over time, becoming more restricted by language and cultural group.

Thus we see one crucial factor is language identity, not established before about the age of 12. A second factor is who the learner has contact with, likely to be with any child at six, more limited to certain children at 12, and fairly restricted in adults. A third factor is the school; usually during the school years, children will be taught through the host community language; after that they will not encounter it in education except if they go to special classes, usually voluntarily.

The importance of making friends outside one's own community cannot be overestimated in this connection. A recent study of immigrants conducted in Dublin primary schools by Lorna Carson and Guus Extra shows that this effect goes in fact beyond the impact of making friends with native speakers of the host country language.[12] Carson and Extra discovered that the 'best friend' factor was highly instrumental in promoting the use of English outside the home as a lingua franca with immigrant children from other communities, and that this pattern of behaviour even spilled over into the use of English with friends from the children's own language groups.

Children's best friends and language use   Box 2.8

The reported choice for English with best friends is particularly high ... [C]hildren select to use English as a lingua franca with children from language backgrounds other than their own, or indeed select to use English with children who share the same other language.... It seems that the shift towards English language use here is located within friendships rather than family connections ... (Carson & Extra 2010, p. 49)[12]

Another recent Dublin study by Svetlana Eriksson on the intergenerational transmission of Russian language and culture in Russian-speaking families in Ireland showed friendship with peers outside the Russian-speaking community to be strongly associated with the use of the principal host country language, English, by children and early adolescents as we see in Box 2.9.[13] To repeat the point made earlier, although such friendships are found to prevail especially in younger age groups, they can more plausibly be related to the degree to which the linguistico-cultural identities of such groups are still open to change, and to their inevitably frequent contact with members of the host community than to biological maturation as such.

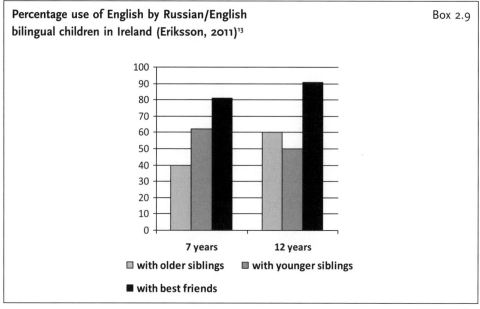

Percentage use of English by Russian/English bilingual children in Ireland (Eriksson, 2011)[13]   Box 2.9

There are also other factors explaining why the immigrant child favours the language of the host country and switches language dominance. For instance, Sandra Kouritzin reports the case of Lara, who had had migrated with her family from Finland to Canada at the age of two, and had subsequently lived for four years in a small town within a tight-knit Finnish community.[14] Lara was thus, until the age of six, a Finnish speaker with very little English. From age six onwards, however, having moved to a large city, and under the influence of her parents' decision that the time had come to integrate with English-speaking Canada, her development in Finnish came to a halt and English progressively took over. Lara reports that the last time she tried (and failed) to converse in Finnish had been when she was 18 years old. Her perception was that she had lost her native language. Here, then, we have an instance of a family taking a decision to opt for one language and effectively to abandon another, with the result that the latter language was lost. The age connection here is again not a matter of maturation as such. In this instance it relates to the fact that parents may make such a choice *for* a child; older immigrants have the power to make such choices for themselves.

Summary: Immigrant children and second language learning   Box 2.10

- a tendency for younger = better;
- the importance of having relationships in the second language;
- links between language and growth of language identity.

The idea of a 'critical period'

The term *critical period* is used in biology to refer to a strictly limited phase in the development of an organism during which a particular competency or behaviour must be acquired if it is to be acquired at all. One often-used example in this connection is imprinting in ducklings and goslings, which, for a short time after hatching, become irreversibly attached to the first moving object they perceive – usually their mother, sometimes a human being – after which they develop a fear of strange objects and retreat instead of following. If language acquisition in human beings is constrained by the limits of a critical period like this, the implication appears to be that, unless language acquisition gets under way before the period ends, it will not happen. There may also be an implication that, even if language acquisition begins within the critical period, it does not continue beyond the end of that period.

Some of the evidence for a critical period in first language acquisition consists of case studies of children who have been isolated from language and brought into contact with it only around the age of puberty, the point which is claimed by some to mark the end of the critical period for language acquisition. Examples of such children are those of Victor, found running wild in the woods of Aveyron in late 18th century France, and Genie, rescued from the isolation imposed by her parents in late 20th century California. Children such as these who are taken into care around puberty typically exhibit some progress in language development – but of a limited kind. Interpretations of such observations vary but it is worth noting that Eric Lenneberg, often called the 'father' of the notion of a critical period in language acquisition (the 'Critical Period Hypothesis') was not convinced of the value of such evidence in relation to his hypothesis, seeing such evidence as interpretable in terms simply of the general damage done to an individual by isolation and cruelty.[15]

> [L]ife in dark closets, wolves' dens, forests or sadistic parents' backyards is not conducive to good health and normal development. (Eric Lenneberg, 1967, p. 142)[15]

Another source of first language evidence sometimes seen as favouring the Critical Period Hypothesis is the mixed success characterizing late acquirers of sign languages. This evidence comes from studies of Deaf subjects who have been deprived of language input in their early years and who then acquire a sign language as their first language at a later age. Such studies do not find that language completely fails to develop but that some deficits are observable in the language of the later signers. Deprivation of language input during the phase in a child's life when cognitive development is at its most intense is likely to have general psychological and cognitive effects; it may be these general effects that are reflected in later language development.

Choice of language   Box 2.11

Who should make the choice of which language a child speaks at home?
    the child   the parents   the state   someone else
Who should make the choice of which language a child speaks at school?
    the child   the parents   the school   the state   someone else
Who should make the choice of which language a child speaks in the local community?
    the child   the parents   the state   someone else

In the second language domain, interpretations of the Critical Period Hypothesis can be summarized as follows: the L2 learner encountering the second language in question after a certain maturational point:

(1) is no longer capable of attaining native-like levels of proficiency in the second language;
(2) and/or needs to expend more conscious effort than is typical of earlier second language acquisition;
(3) and/or makes use of different mechanisms from those deployed in second language acquisition during childhood.

All interpretations converge on the claim that the L2 learner coming to grips with the language beyond a particular maturational stage exhibits a sharp decline in second learning potential as compared with younger learners.

With regard to the first point, the suitability of applying the native-speaker criterion to L2 learners is questioned elsewhere in this book, for example in Topic 8. Nevertheless the criterion has long been used in the Critical Period Hypothesis literature and continues to be used. The idea that late L2 learners cannot achieve native-like levels of second language proficiency has in any case been undermined by a large number of studies, including Ciara Kinsella's work.[16] This involved 20 native English speakers who had been raised monolingually, who had not begun learning French before the age of 11 and whose average age of significant exposure to French (namely arrival in France) was 28.6 years. All were resident in France, and all reported at least occasionally passing for native speakers of French. These participants (and a control group of native French speakers) were asked to identify some regional French accents and to complete a test incorporating lexical and grammatical elements. Three of the 20 participants scored within native-speaker ranges on all tasks (outperforming many of the native speakers on the accent recognition task). In the face of such findings, it is sometimes claimed that there is no recorded case of a post-pubertal second language beginner behaving *in every last detail* like a native speaker. This is no doubt true, but why should we expect otherwise? The fact is that the more closely we scrutinize the second language performance of individuals whose exposure to the second language began very early, the more we find that they too differ at the level of fine linguistic detail from monoglot native speakers.

> **Puberty and language** Box 2.12
>
> The incidence of 'language learning blocks' rapidly increases after puberty. Also automatic acquisition from mere exposure to a given language seems to disappear after this age, and foreign languages have to be taught and learned through a conscious and labored effort. (Eric Lenneberg, 1967)[15]

With reference to the alleged effortfulness of later language learning, this goes back to the very beginnings of the Critical Period Hypothesis and continues to recur in recent discussions of the topic. The suggestion that conscious effort is absolutely indispensable for high levels of attainment in late L2 learning is, however, questionable. Georgette Ioup investigated two extremely successful adult users of Egyptian Arabic, one of whom was untutored.[17] This untutored late learner was found to perform in Arabic in a native-like manner even in areas of which she was unaware – e.g. subtle aspects of syntax and pronunciation. One might add that even if later second language learning *is* more 'conscious and labored', this may have nothing to do with the ending of a critical period specifically related to language. After all, the conscious, deliberate dimension tends to increase in *all* areas of learning as cognitive development advances.

> **Different views on access to Universal Grammar (UG) in late learners**
> (based on Mitchell & Myles, 2004[18]; Cook, 1985[19]) Box 2.13
>
> (1) *No access hypothesis*: UG is not involved in late L2 acquisition; late L2 learners have to resort to more general problem-solving skills.
> (2) *Full access hypothesis*: UG is accessed directly in early and late L2 acquisition; L1 and L2 acquisition are basically similar processes, the differences observed being due to the difference in cognitive maturity and in learner needs.
> (3) *Indirect access hypothesis*: UG is not directly involved in late L2 acquisition, but it is indirectly accessed via the L1; therefore, there will be just one instantiation (i.e. one working example) of UG available to the L2 learner, with the parameters fixed to the L1 settings.
> (4) *Partial access hypothesis*: some aspects of UG are still available and others not; this approach takes UG and its various subcomponents as the starting point, hypothesising that some submodules of UG are more or less accessible to the L2 learner.

The idea that children and adults may have qualitatively different language-learning mechanisms at their disposal has been interpreted in a particular way by some researchers working within a Chomskyan framework, who have taken the view that post-pubertal second language learning is not underpinned by the innate bioprogamming provided by 'Universal Grammar' (UG). The UG model claims that essential parts of language are not acquired but built-in to the human mind and has led to lively arguments for and against the innateness of language in the mind. It has been widely suggested that late L2 learners do not seem to exhibit grammars that are not sanctioned by UG, and that post-pubertal L2 learners appear to deal in the same manner as L1 acquirers with linguistic features supposedly having a UG basis. For example L2 users show they know the principle of structure-dependency which rules out sentences like *Is Sam is the cat that black?* (only the *is* in the main clause can be moved) just as much as L1 children, even though they are unlikely to have been taught the principle or to have encountered any examples of it.[20]

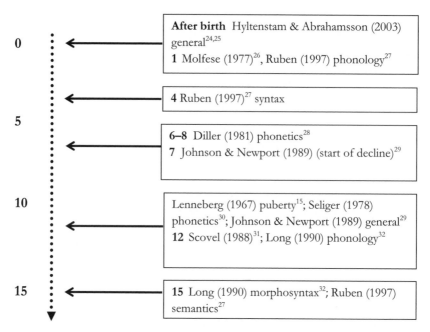

Figure 2.1 *Different endpoints assigned to the critical period by researchers*

Another approach to the question of maturationally induced changes in underlying language learning mechanisms is that of Robert DeKeyser.[21] Implicit learning where people learn unconsciously and automatically is often contrasted with explicit learning in which people learn consciously with deliberate attention. DeKeyser looked at L2 learners whose second language experience had begun in their childhood and adult years respectively. DeKeyser claimed that the adult beginners who scored within the range of the child beginners had high levels of verbal analytical ability, an ability which seemed to play no role in the performance of the child beginners. His interpretation was that maturational constraints apply only to implicit language learning mechanisms; adults can employ explicit learning where children rely on implicit learning. Other researchers commenting on similar findings point to the possible influence of primary versus secondary-level instructional styles and to the possibility that such results reflect general cognitive changes, which impact on language learning, but on other areas of development too.

Turning now to the question of whether there is a sharp decline in second language-acquiring capacity at some stage in maturation, findings from studies investigating 'naturalistic' L2 acquisition, as we have seen, favour the notion that, while adolescent and adult subjects may have an initial advantage, in the long run younger beginners are more likely to attain very high levels of proficiency. On the other hand, research into primary-level second language programmes in schools yields a rather different picture, which we shall explore further in the next section. The evidence does not, in any case, support the simplistic 'younger = better in all circumstances over any timescale' perspective which underlay some early treatments. Even in the 'naturalistic' context, the age of first encounter seems to be only one of the determinants of the ultimate level of proficiency attained. There is also a question mark over the notion that any such age-related decline has a so-called 'elbow' or '7' shape of the kind that one would expect if a critical period were its cause. In recent years new research and also some re-analysis of earlier research suggest a gradual decline similar to that which characterises learning capacity in general. According to Ellen Bialystok's reading of recent findings, 'the tendency for proficiency to decline with age projects well into adulthood and does not mark some defined change in learning potential at around puberty'[22] and, according to David Birdsong's interpretation, age-related decline in this context is captured by 'a linear function'.[23]

In sum, it appears that any age-related decline in second language-learning capacity varies from person to person and from one aspect of language to another, which is not what one would expect if its underlying cause were an inevitable critical period in human development.

> [T]he end of the critical period for language in humans has proven ... difficult to find, with estimates ranging from 1 year of age to adolescence. (p. 285)[33]

It also appears that any decline in second language-learning capacity with age is continuous and linear, which, again, is not in keeping with the usual understanding of the notion of critical period.

Finally, so far we have been talking about the Critical Period Hypothesis as if it were a single proposal. This is actually far from the case. There is such a variety of proposals that we should really be talking about the Critical Period Hypotheses. For example, with regard to the offset point or endpoint of the critical period, although puberty is (following Lenneberg) often mentioned in this regard, other suggestions for the age effect abound, as seen in Figure 2.1. The impact of such uncertainty is twofold.

First, it undermines the plausibility of the whole notion of a critical period for language acquisition; and second, it deprives the concepts of 'early' and 'late' L2 learning of any kind of stable reference point and therefore meaning.

With regard to the first remark above, if there were clear evidence of an offset point for a window of opportunity for language aquisition, surely it ought to be possible for researchers to agree where it is situated.

Two views of age and classroom language learning Box 2.14

If the goal for learning/teaching a foreign language is to obtain the highest level of second language skills ... there is support for the argument that 'earlier is better'. This support, found in the critical period hypothesis literature, is based on the claim that biological and maturational factors constrain language learning beyond a certain age.[34]

[T]he learning which occurs in the formal language classroom may be unlike the learning which occurs during immersion, such that early instruction does not necessarily have the advantage for ultimate performance that is held by early immersion. (p. 81)[29]

The fact of such wide *dis*agreement about this matter can be taken to cast severe doubt on the whole notion of a critical period for language. Concerning the stability of reference points, if 12 *years* is taken to be the critical age, L2 learning at age four is presumably 'early' learning; if 12 *months* is taken to be the critical age, on the other hand, then L2 learning at the age of four is already 'late' learning. Nor does variability in views on the critical period concern only the timing of its ending; it also relates to the scope of critical period effects. Whereas, for example, Eric Lenneberg saw maturational constraints as affecting language in general, for Tom Scovel they are relevant only to the phonetic/phonological sphere.

The effects of early instruction in a second language

There seems to be quite a widespread assumption that the kinds of younger = better tendencies that we observe among 'naturalistic' L2 learners operate also in formal instructional settings, that is to say the teaching of second languages in schools. There also seems to be a widely held view that the degree of success of L2 learning in formal instructional settings is so much bound up with the maturational factor that almost no other factors are relevant.

Concerning the first point above, the studies involving subjects who have been learning second languages in formal instructional settings yield a different pattern to that obtained in naturalistic settings. That is to say, such research has confirmed the finding related to the faster rate of older starters but has not confirmed the long-term benefits of an early start when younger and older starters have had the same number of hours of instruction.[35,36]

Carmen Muñoz argues that in a typical instructed setting, where the second language is treated as one subject among many, the expectation that younger starters will in the long term outperform older starters after the same amount of hours or courses of instruction is not warranted.[37-39] Her reasoning is that while young children may be superior to older learners at implicit learning, implicit learning requires massive amounts of input that a typical foreign language setting does not provide; and that in regard to older learners, these seem to be superior to young children at explicit learning for which the classroom setting provides many opportunities.

It is true that some SLA researchers who subscribe to the Critical Period Hypothesis have no hesitation in claiming that it constitutes an argument for early second language instruction. Other Critical Period Hypothesis advocates, however, take a different line. Jacqueline Johnson and Elissa Newport note that the crucial measure in their research was age of arrival in the second language environment rather than age of onset of formal second language instruction.[29] Robert DeKeyser (see above) agrees.[21] For him, school-based L2 learning is typically explicit in nature and largely unaffected by maturational constraints.

Interestingly, just as there are supporters of the Critical Period Hypothesis who do not necessarily argue for early second language instruction, there are Critical Period Hypothesis sceptics who are all in favour of the introduction of second languages into the primary school curriculum. Researchers such as Evelyn Hatch[40] and Fred Genesee[41] have argued for early second language instruction on grounds not of maturational constraints but of factors such as the general desirability of as long an exposure to the second language as possible and the importance of laying an early foundation to L2 learning so that ground can covered later that might otherwise be neglected.

In any case, since the 1990s throughout Europe and indeed across the world, there has been a clear and accelerating trend towards the introduction of additional languages into primary-level curricula, as seen in Figure 2.2. This trend appears often to have been underlain by the widespread belief on the part of parents – whose views feed into the

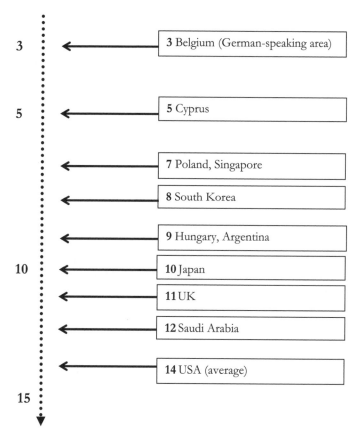

Figure 2.2 *Ages at which children start learning second languages in different countries (as compiled in 2013)*

decisions of governments – that an early start in second language instruction is a panacea overriding and neutralising all other factors.

We might do well in this connection to recall John T. Bruer's wise comment that one of the dangers of focusing on maturational issues in discussing learning is that it prompts us to pay too much attention to *when* learning occurs and too little attention to the *conditions* of learning.[42]

If we have need of sobering exemplification and illustration in this connection, we could do worse than look closely at the teaching of the Irish language in the Republic of Ireland. In the Republic of Ireland, Irish is taught as part of the core primary curriculum from the infant grades onwards. This has been the situation virtually since the foundation of the Irish state. The inclusion of Irish in the primary school curriculum was based on notions of recovering and revitalising it as a marker of Irish national identity. Only a tiny proportion of the population of the country are native speakers of Irish (although the exact figure is controversial), and so for the vast majority of pupils in Irish schools Irish constitutes an additional language. What is the outcome of this almost century-long experiment in early second language instruction? In a word, disappointing. Kevin Myers declared in *The Irish Independent* on October 3, 2011:

> The 'restoration' of spoken Irish is the greatest single economic and cultural project in the history of the State. Not merely has it been the greatest national failure, but it has also revealed a national disorder; the acceptance of a consensual falsehood across society, from the intimate disclosures of a census form to the public formulation of national policy.

This is the view not only of controversialist journalists like Kevin Myers but also of successive Irish Language Commissioners and the present Irish Minister for Education.

It has to be acknowledged that the conditions under which Irish has been taught have not been ideal – in terms of the teaching materials and teaching methodologies deployed, in terms of teacher motivation and proficiency, and in terms of societal attitudes; but this is precisely the point – an early start to instruction in the language has failed to trump such unpromising conditions. The lesson to be learned from the case of Irish is this: starting second language instruction early does not absolve us from paying very close attention indeed to optimising the circumstances under which teaching and learning proceed. If such circumstances are unfavourable, the age factor will not rescue the situation, whose outcome may be indifferent or even disastrous.

Summary: The Critical Period Hypothesis Box 2.15

- Associated originally with Eric Lenneberg's suggestion that normal L1 acquisition ceases in the early teens.
- Supported by evidence that language-deprived children do not acquire normal language if rescued in their teens, whether 'wolf' children or deaf children not exposed to a sign language.
- In the second language, the Critical Period Hypothesis claims L2 learners past a certain age do not achieve 'native-like' competence, need to work harder and use different types of learning.
- These claims may well be true but there is no reason why the achievements of L2 learning should be the same as L1 acquisition, given the presence of a second language in the mind.
- Multiple ages have been postulated for the end of the Critical Period in L2 acquisition and for different aspects of language.
- In general, educational systems in many countries increasingly tend to teach a second language earlier rather than later.

Some concluding remarks

Age is clearly a factor in second language learning, as it is in all other learning. There are in addition some not strictly maturational age-*related* factors that play a role in second language learning – factors such as what kind of language education (if any) is readily available when one enters the second language environment. These considerations argue in favour of childhood being the most favourable time to begin to be exposed to a second language, at least in 'naturalistic' circumstances.

As far as instruction in a second language is concerned, the situation is distinctly complex. An early start in this context does not seem necessarily to advantage the recipients. It would seem wise, when the introduction of early second language instruction is being contemplated, for a very wide spectrum of considerations to be taken account of – much wider than the question of age. An unfortunate outcome of a bad set of educational decisions in this matter will certainly not be salvaged by the age factor.

The general point to be emphasised is that, given motivation and perseverance, good results in second language learning can in fact be achieved at any age.

Postscript Box 2.16

Having read the chapter would you now recommend people should start learning another language before 10/between 10 and 15/after 15/at any age?

Or would you say the answer is meaningless if it does not take into account the circumstances of the learner and the aspect of language involved?

Further reading

Very different perspectives on the age factor in second language learning are taken in the following two books:

Herschensohn, J. (2007) *Language Development and Age*. Cambridge: Cambridge University Press.

Singleton, D. and Ryan, L. (2004) *Language Acquisition: The Age Factor*, 2nd edition. Clevedon: Multilingual Matters.

A fascinating collection of material on various aspects of the immigrant experience in relation to language learning is to be found in:

Kondo-Brown, K. (2006) *Heritage Language Development: Focus on East Asian Immigrants*. Amsterdam: John Benjamins.

A wide-ranging treatment of factors in the development of bilingualism and multilingualism – including some sidelights on age-related issues – is offered by:

Auer, P. and Li Wei (eds) (2007) *Handbook of Multilingualism and Multilingual Communication*. Berlin: Mouton de Gruyter.

The educational dimension of early second language learning is comprehensively addressed in:

Nikolov, M. (2009) *The Age Factor and Early Language Learning*. Berlin: Walter de Gruyter.

References

1. Tomb, J.W. (1925) On the intuitive capacity of children to understand spoken languages. *British Journal of Psychology* 16, 53–54.

2. Rokita, J. (2006) Comparing early L2 lexical development in naturalistic and instructional settings. In J. Leśniewska and E. Witalisz (eds) (2006) *Language and Identity: English and American Studies in the Age of Globalization*. Krakow: Jagiellonian University Press, 70–82.

3. Brändle, M. (1986) Language teaching for the 'young-old'. *Babel* 21 (1), 17–21.

4. Asher, J. and Garcia, R. (1969) The optimal age to learn a foreign language. *Modern Language Journal* 53 (5), 334–341.

5. Seliger, H., Krashen, S. and Ladefoged P. (1975) Maturational constraints in the acquisition of second language accent. *Language Sciences* 36, 20–22.

6. Patkowski, M.S. (1980) The sensitive period for the acquisition of syntax in a second language. *Language Learning* 30 (2), 449–472.

7. Hyltenstam, K. (1992) Non-native features of non-native speakers: On the ultimate attainment of childhood L2 learners. In R.J. Harris (ed.) (1992) *Cognitive Processing in Bilinguals*. New York: Elsevier, 351–368.

8. Piske, T., Flege, J.E., MacKay, I.R.A. and Meador, D. (2002) The production of English vowels by fluent early and late Italian-English bilinguals. *Phonetica* 59 (1), 49–71.

9. Snow, C. and Hoefnagel-Höhle, M. (1978) The critical period for language acquisition: Evidence from second language learning. *Child Development* 49 (4), 1114–1128.

10. Jia, G. and Aaronson, D. (1999) Age differences in second language acquisition. The dominant language switch and maintenance hypothesis. *Proceedings of the 23rd Annual Boston University Conference on Language Development*, 301–312. Sommerville MA: Cascadilla.

11. Bialystok, E. (1997) The structure of age: In search of barriers to second language acquisition. *Second Language Research* 13 (2), 116–137.

12. Carson, L. and Extra, G. (2010) Multilingualism in Dublin: Home Language Use Among Primary School Children. Report on a Pilot Survey. Dublin: Trinity College, Centre for Language and Communication Studies.

13. Eriksson, S. (2011) Family and Migration: The Intergenerational Transmission of Culture, Language and Ethnic Identification in Russian-Speaking Families in the Republic of Ireland. PhD thesis. Trinity College Dublin.

14. Kouritzin, S.G. (1999) *Face(t)s of First Language Loss*. Mahwah, NJ: Lawrence Erlbaum.

15. Lenneberg, E.H. (1967) *Biological Foundations of Language*. New York: Wiley.

16. Kinsella, C. (2009) An Investigation into the Proficiency of Successful Late Learners of French. PhD thesis. Trinity College Dublin.

17. Ioup, G. (1995) Evaluating the need for input enhancement in post-critical period language acquisition. In D. Singleton and Z. Lengyel (eds) (1995) *The Age Factor in Second Language Acquisition*. Clevedon: Multilingual Matters, 95–123.

18. Mitchell, R. and Myles. F. (2004) *Second Language Learning Theories*, 2nd edition. London: Arnold.

19. Cook, V.J. (1985) Chomsky's Universal Grammar and second language learning. *Applied Linguistics* 6, 1–8.

20. Cook, V.J. (2003) The poverty-of-the-stimulus argument and structure-dependency in L2 users of English. *International Review of Applied Linguistics* 41, 201–221.

21. DeKeyser, R. (2000) The robustness of critical period effects in second language acquisition. *Studies in Second Language Acquisition* 22 (4), 499–533.

22. Bialystok, E. and Hakuta, K. (1999) Confounded age: Linguistic and cognitive factors in age. In D. Birdsong (ed.) (1999) *Second Language Acquisition and the Critical Period Hypothesis*. Mahwah, NJ: Erlbaum, 161–181.

23. Birdsong, D. (2006) Age and second language acquisition and processing: A selective overview. *Language Learning* 56 (1), 9–49.

24. Hyltenstam, K. and Abrahamsson, N. (2003) Maturational constraints in SLA. In C. Doughty and M.H. Long (eds) (2003) *The Handbook of Second Language Acquisition*. Malden, MA: Blackwell, 539–588.

25. Hyltenstam, K. and Abrahamsson, N. (2003) Age de l'exposition initiale et niveau terminal chez les locuteurs du suédois L2. *Acquisition et Interaction en Langue Étrangère* 18, 99–127.

26. Molfese, D. (1977) Infant cerebral asymmetry. In S.J. Segalowitz and F.A. Gruber (eds) (1977) *Language Development and Neurological Theory*. New York: Academic Press, 22–37.

27. Ruben, R.J. (1997) A time frame of critical/sensitive periods of language development. *Acta Otolaryngologica* 117 (2), 202–205.

28. Diller, K.C. (ed.) (1981) *Individual Differences and Universals in Language Learning*. Rowley, MA: Newbury House.

29. Johnson, J.S. and Newport, E.L. (1989) Critical period effects in second language learning: The influence of maturational state on the acquisition of ESL. *Cognitive Psychology* 21 (1), 60–99.

30. Seliger, H.W. (1978) Implications of a multiple critical periods hypothesis for second language learning. In W.C. Ritchie (ed.) (1978) *SLA Research: Issues and Implications*. New York: Academic Press, 11–19.

31. Scovel, T. (1988) *A Time to Speak: A Psycholinguistic Inquiry into the Critical Period for Human Language*. Rowley, MA: Newbury House.

32. Long, M.H. (1990) Maturational constraints on language development. *Studies in Second Language Acquisition* 12 (3), 251–285.

33. Aram, D., Bates, E., Eisele, J., Fenson, J., Nass, R., Thal, D. and Trauner, D. (1997) From first words to grammar in children with focal brain injury. *Developmental Neuropsychology* 13 (3), 275–343.

34. Spada, N. (2004) Interview. *ReVEL – Revista Virtual de Estudos de Linguagem* 2 (2). http://planeta.terra.com.br/educacao/revel/edicoes/num_2/interview_l2.htm.

35. Singleton, D. and Muñoz, C. (2011) Around and beyond the Critical Period Hypothesis. In E. Hinkel (ed.) (2011) *Handbook of Research in Second Language Teaching and Learning: Volume II*, 407–425. London: Routledge.

36. Muñoz, C. and Singleton, D. (2011) A critical review of age-related research on L2 ultimate attainment: State of the Art article. *Language Teaching* 44 (1), 1–35.

37. Muñoz, C. (2006) The effects of age on foreign language learning: The BAF Project. In C. Muñoz (ed.) (2006) *Age and the Rate of Foreign Language Learning*. Clevedon: Multilingual Matters, 1–40.

38. Muñoz, C. (2008a) Symmetries and asymmetries of age effects in naturalistic and instructed L2. *Applied Linguistics* 24 (4), 578–596.

39. Muñoz, C. (2008b) Age-related differences in foreign language learning. Revisiting the empirical evidence. *International Review of Applied Linguistics in Language Teaching* 46 (3), 197–220.

40. Hatch, E. (1983) *Psycholinguistics: A Second Language Perspective*. Rowley, MA: Newbury House.

41. Genesee, F. (1978) Is there an optimal age for starting second language instruction? *McGill Journal of Education* 13, 145–154.

42. Bruer, J.T. (1999) *The Myth of The First Three Years: A New Understanding of Early Brain Development and Lifelong Learning*. New York: Free Press.

3

How Do People Acquire the Words of a Second Language?

David Singleton

Starter: What's a word?   Box 3.1

Is a word just a 'sequence of letters without any spaces' (Hurford)?[1] Or do you have a better definition?

How important are words in language?

If you know a word like *bug*, what things do you know about it?

Words and more

Words are obviously a vital element of language, and there is a widespread strong association between the concept of word and that of language. In some languages the very term for 'word' indeed also has the sense of 'speech' or 'talk'. We can refer in this context also to the English expression *to have a word with someone*, which obviously means having a talk with someone rather that just uttering a single word to someone. Nor is awareness of words confined to literate societies and individuals. The linguist Edward Sapir, conducting fieldwork on Native American languages in the 1920s, found that although the Native Americans he was working with were illiterate, and thus unaccustomed to the concept of the written word, they nevertheless had no serious difficulty in dictating a text to him word by word, and that they were also quite capable of isolating particular words and repeating them as units.[2] Indeed, according to Eve Clark and Elaine Andersen, children have a very early awareness of words, correcting themselves when they make errors with words before they start self-correcting the structure of their sentences.[4]

Words meaning both 'word' and 'speech'/'talk'   Box 3.2

Chinese *yán* Italian *parola* Japanese *kotoba* Turkish *laf* French *parole* Spanish *palabra* Modern Greek *léxi*

Central though the concept of word may be, defining it is far from straightforward. Words may be thought of as particular recognised sound-shapes or written forms – 'Shakespeare had a vocabulary of about 60,000 words' – or as individual occurrences of such forms – 'Shakespeare's *Hamlet* is about 33,500 words long'; they may be considered from a strictly formal point of view or from a more abstract perspective; or they may be characterised in terms of different linguistic 'levels' – orthographic, phonological, semantic or grammatical. Defining the area of language where words belong, widely referred to as the *lexicon*, is even more problematic. In any practical dictionary, the material provided under each word entry contains far more than a specification of form and meaning. Take the abbreviated entry for *kettle* seen in Box 3.3: it includes, among other things, grammatical information – *kettle* is an 'n', i.e. a noun – and phonological information – it is pronounced /ket(ə)l/. But also in many cases it includes information about geographical use – *solicitor* in British English means a kind of lawyer, in American

English someone who solicits – and stylistic information – *kettle* meaning 'criminal' is marked as slang. In the same way the lexicon of any language that we 'carry round in our heads', our *mental lexicon*, consists of more than just an inventory of forms and meanings. The reason for this is simply that the use of any given word takes account of and has repercussions for a wide variety of dimensions of the language we interpret and produce in any given environment.

A sample dictionary entry, highly abbreviated from the *Oxford English Dictionary*[3]

Box 3.3

kettle, n.
Pronunciation: /ket(ə)l/
Etymology: Common Germanic: Old English *cetel* . . .
1.
   a. A vessel, commonly of metal, for boiling water or other liquids over a fire; a pot or caldron . . .); now *esp.* a covered metal vessel with a spout, used to boil water for domestic purposes, a tea-kettle n.
   b. A bowl- or saucer-shaped vessel in which operations are carried out on low-melting metals, glass, plastics, etc., in the liquid state . . .

However, while the concept of the word is crucial, some entries in the lexicon are longer than words, such as verb-preposition combinations, *look up/look out/look in/look out for/look up to*, etc. Hence the contents of the mental lexicon are sometimes more technically known as 'lexical items' or 'lexical entries', which are not necessarily quite the same as words.

What does it mean to know a word?

Box 3.4

Is knowing a word being able to recognize what it sounds like and looks like? Is it being able to give the word's dictionary definition? Research suggests . . . *no*. Knowing a word by sight and sound and knowing its dictionary definition are not the same as knowing how to use the word . . . and understanding it when it is heard or seen in various contexts. (Lehr, Osborn and Hiebert, 2004)[5]

Obviously, language users need to know the pronunciation of a word and (in literate societies) its written form; but they need to know a great deal more than that – including the various kinds of meanings it can and cannot convey, how it relates to and combines with other words, the effects of different contexts on its usage and impact, the extent of its use (international-national-regional-local-individual), the level of use (cultivated-general-uncultivated) and its typical register(s) (formal-informal-familiar). Thus, when we look closely at what is involved in the knowledge of any given word, wider issues immediately have to come into consideration.

Take the unremarkable word *bug*, for instance. As soon as we home in on this word, we note that some dimensions of its profile are that:

- it can function as both a noun and a verb; *a bug/to bug*;
- as well as 'insect', it has a range of meanings based on metaphorical extensions: e.g. 'annoy' (*She really bugs me*), 'infectious illness' (*Jane is down with a stomach bug*), 'fault'

(*This software is full of bugs*), 'enthusiastic interest' (*My son really has the golf bug*), 'concealed microphone' (*The journalist had planted a bug in his telephone*);
- it participates in commonly occurring expressions such as *litter bug, snug as a bug in a rug*;
- some of its senses are more appropriate in informal rather than formal contexts – *you're bugging me*;
- some of its uses are confined to one part of the world, for example *fire-bug* in the USA and Canada.

So the mental lexicon is a good deal more interesting than simply a mental list of words. Research shows that our use of the dictionaries on our bookshelves is on the whole rather conservative. Most of us consult dictionaries just to check spellings and meanings, largely ignoring all the rich grammatical, stylistic, etc. information that dictionary entries provide. With regard to the mental lexicon, however, accessing and using the whole range of information it contains is vital for the accuracy of our understanding of and the appropriateness of our responses to what we encounter in our interactions in and with language in our daily life. The construction of this rich and complex body of knowledge and processes is clearly a challenge, whether in the acquiring of a language in infancy or in the learning of a second language in later years. This challenge is what we now turn to.

Words and concepts Box 3.5

Can you separate the concepts in your mind from your words? Are there concepts for which you don't have words? Or are there indeed words for which you don't have concepts?

Are concepts like 'table' or 'movement' common to all human beings? If so, is this because of the way their minds work or their common experiences with the world around them?

Summary Box 3.6

- Words form lexical entries in a large mental lexicon in everybody's mind.
- A lexical entry includes many aspects of each word, including their pronunciation and spelling, their grammatical use, their meaning, their role phrases, their appropriateness of use, etc.

The lexical challenge in infancy ... and later

According to Chomsky, among others, the rate of vocabulary acquisition in infancy is so rapid and precise that the obvious conclusion is that we are born with a set of concepts to which we simply have to attach names: '... the concepts are already available ... the child's task is to assign labels to concepts' (p. 61).[6] There are some problems with this view. Chief among these perhaps is the fact that different languages and cultures configure concepts in the words they use in radically divergent ways, so that to think of lexical development in terms of assigning labels to pre-existent universal concepts is, at best, a simplification. Another objection is that young children's engagement with words is not actually as fast or as straightforward as Chomsky implies. In fact it seems to be something of a struggle and in the early stages distinctly sluggish.

Moreover, the child's road to conventional meanings has many a twist and turn. His/her early meanings may be vague and fluid and they may be over-extended or under-extended relative to adult usage. One child may use *pussy-cat* to refer to all animals regardless of species (over-extension), another may use *pussy-cat* to refer to their family pet (under-extension) but not to the cat next door. It is true that once 30 or so items have been internalised the rate of acquisition tends to accelerate, as we see in the typical 'vocabulary explosion' around 16 months, as seen in Box 3.7, especially in respect of labels for objects, which some research suggests is connected to the fact that such words are easier to 'picture' than others. However, there follows a long period of revision, reorganisation and consolidation of lexical knowledge, which has its onset in the pre-school period but at least in some of its aspects seems to continue right through schooling.

American English children's early words
Months Words   Box 3.7

Months	Words
12	daddy, mommy
13	bye
14	dog, hi
15	baby, ball, no
16	banana, eye, nose, bottle, juice, bird, duck, cookie, woof, moo, ouch, baabaaa, night night, book, balloon, boat
17	cracker, apple, cheese, ear, keys, bath, peekaboo, vroom, up, down
18	grandma, grandpa, sock, hat, truck, boat, thank you, cat

The months show the age at which 50% of children say a particular word.

'[C]hildren's first 50 words fall into a fairly small number of categories . . .: people, food, body-parts, clothing, animals, vehicles, toys, household objects, routines and activities or states'. (Clark 2009, p. 76)[7]

Whether or not there is an innate dimension to the process of mastering vocabulary, some features of linguistic communication between adults and young children may assist the child's progress in this area. One such feature is the way in which such communication focuses on things, people, events, etc., in the 'here and now'. The early vocabulary of young children is indeed largely composed of items that relate to their everyday circumstances and activities. As we see in the box, they talk about bananas and grandmas, not income tax or aubergines. Another relevant feature of adults' communication with young children is the adults' use of 'ostensive definition'; that is to say, they define words by pointing at the relevant objects or activities and naming them. Unlike other aspects of child-directed communication, which are essentially oriented towards helping the child to understand, ostension appears to be a kind of informal 'teaching' on the part of caregivers: *Look at that – it's a hippopotamus!*

Although a very large number and wide variety of cultures around the world – including sign language using deaf cultures – exhibit these kinds of features of adult-child communication, not all do. Some middle-class parents in England have claimed to reject any simplification of language addressed to children such as baby-talk. Researchers such as Noam Chomsky[6] and Stephen Pinker[8] have therefore argued that such features cannot be absolutely *necessary* for language development since not all children encounter them. Even if features of child-directed communication like 'here and now' orientation and ostension are not strictly indispensable for lexical development, there is little doubt that they facilitate it.

Once a certain number of words have been acquired, the child is obviously in a position not only to associate newly encountered forms with entities, attributes and processes to which they are applied, but also to attempt meaning associations between new items and already internalised words which resemble them in form. I can cite an example of this from the early lexical acquisition of one of my own sons, who on encountering the word *porcupine* in the context of a picture-book that was being read to him made an astute but mistaken connection between the first part of the word and the verb *to prick* and coded the word (and thereafter for a time produced it) as *prickypine*.

So how relevant is lexical development in a first language for second language lexical development? Obviously, first language and second language learners differ in at least two major ways. To begin with, L2 learners are usually at more advanced stages in cognitive terms. In addition, L2 learners have already been through the process of language acquisition. There is no question of L2 learners having to re-traverse the cooing and babbling stages of first language developments; their utterances in the second language are more or less from the outset comprised of combinations of meaningful elements. Also, the L2 learner at some level already knows about the labelling function of words and the kinds of ways in which they may relate to each other.

It was noted above that some theorists see lexical development in infancy as relying on the existence of innate concepts. If such innate concepts are indeed a reality, it is not clear whether L2 learners also have access to them – at least beyond a certain age. We see in the chapter on age that those who favour the view that language acquisition is shaped and helped along by innate endowments disagree over the extent to which such biologically endowed elements and mechanisms remain available to L2 learners beyond the childhood years – the critical period hypothesis. As we have seen, infant language acquirers may be assisted by the particular characteristics of child-directed communication. Similarly, L2 learners may receive some help from the ways in which they are addressed by native speakers of their target language.

Translation equivalents?   Box 3.8

English *bite* and French *mordre* correspond closely when they refer to cutting with teeth, but outside this use they go their separate ways: one is *piqué*, not *mordu*, by a mosquito, while *la balle a mordu la ligne* means *the ball just touched the line*. (Swan 1997)[9]

Such 'foreigner talk' or 'foreigner register' has been observed in a number of studies to be, among other things, lexically more restricted than linguistic interaction between native speakers and to include ostensive gestures and other definitions of one kind and another. Similar kinds of input tuning are also apparently typical of 'teacher talk' in second language classrooms, with simplification of vocabulary and high use of *right, ah* and *okay*. The vocabulary-related features of foreigner talk are summed up in Box 3.9.

Features of foreigner talk — Box 3.9

High frequency vocabulary
- Less slang.
- Fewer idioms.

Fewer pronoun forms

Definitions
- Overtly marked (e.g. *This means X*).
- Semantic feature information (e.g. *a cathedral usually means a church, that's a very high ceiling*).
- Contextual information (e.g. *if you go for a job in a factory, they talk about a wage scale*).
- Gestures and pictures. (Gass and Selinker 2008, p. 306)[10]

The fact that L2 learners already have a body of first language lexical knowledge at their disposal means that the possibilities for making semantic associations between lexical items – of the kind noted for first language acquisition – extend to the making of associations between second language and first language words. Such associations are certainly attempted by L2 learners – even if the first and second language are totally unrelated. For example, it has been shown that native speakers of Hebrew learning English, an unrelated language, make such associations between Hebrew words and English words, some examples of which are seen in Box 3.10. This kind of process often extends to the creation of forms which are not recognised by native speakers of the second language as words of their language. For instance, an English-speaking learner

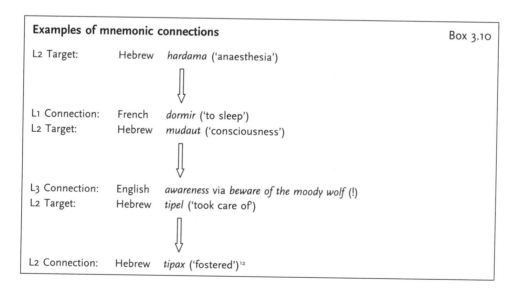

Examples of mnemonic connections — Box 3.10

L2 Target:	Hebrew	*hardama* ('anaesthesia')

⇓

L1 Connection:	French	*dormir* ('to sleep')
L2 Target:	Hebrew	*mudaut* ('consciousness')

⇓

L3 Connection:	English	*awareness* via *beware of the moody wolf* (!)
L2 Target:	Hebrew	*tipel* ('took care of')

⇓

L2 Connection:	Hebrew	*tipax* ('fostered')[12]

of French, having successfully made connections between the forms and meanings of French *actif, impulsif, intensif* and, respectively, English *active, impulsive, intensive*, is very likely to assume that the relevant 'conversion rules' always work and to produce a (non-French) form like *expensif* when confronted with the need to render English *expensive*.[13]

L2 learners clearly start from further down the road of exploring meaning than infants confronting the task of first language acquisition. Indeed, many of the meanings and meaning hierarchies needed for second language use will have already been internalised in the first language context, and will be recyclable with only minimal adjustment in the second language.

On the other hand, whatever the degree of 'cultural overlap' between two language communities, there will always be areas and items of meaning which do not correspond. In some instances the L2 learner is faced with concepts for which no words exist in their native language. More often the meanings of the second language are differently structured and distributed compared with those of the first language. It is hardly surprising, in such circumstances, if lexical fluidity, over-extension and under-extension occur in second language development just as they do in first language acquisition – in the second language case, the process of coming to grips with the semantic range of newly encountered words being constrained and shaped by the experience the L2 learner has had of the word itself, of related words and of the relevant conceptual domain.

In L2 learning, as in first language development, words that are easy to imagine seem to be more readily learnable than words that are less easy to 'see' mentally; it's easier to remember the word *horse* than the word *generalise*. In the 1990s Nick Ellis interpreted many of the findings arising from second language lexical research in this way,[14] and Brian Tomlinson argued for the general value of visualisation in second language vocabulary learning.[15] Tomlinson showed in his own research that second language readers who visualise retain more of the texts they read (including individual words) than those who do not.

Learning new words   Box 3.11

Try to remember 10 Italian words, taken from a beginners' course *Italian Now*[16]:

> antipatico 'disagreeable', fermasi 'to stop', pigro 'lazy', anello 'ring', ogni 'every', faccia 'face', bancarella 'stall', pesante 'tiresome', aprirsi 'to open', scontrino 'receipt'

How did you go about learning them? Did it vary according to the type of word?

Summary   Box 3.12

- L1 children's lexical development is partly the result of specialised linguistic interaction with their parents and the environment around them, partly the result of the natural predispositions in their minds.
- L2 learners also may encounter specialised language and benefit from words with concrete meanings.
- L2 learners may in addition form links between the L1 and L2 words.

Learning words one at a time

Second language researchers sometimes give the impression that there is a conflict between those who subscribe to the view that L2 learners need to focus on the memorisation of individual lexical expressions, what one might call the 'atomistic' approach, and those who adopt a perspective which relies on the assumption that new vocabulary will be picked up in context, 'incidentally', through interaction in the second language, reading passages, etc., without deliberate memorisation being involved. In fact, the consensus among researchers is that – as anyone who has ever learnt or taught a second language will readily agree – context-based and atomistic lexical learning both have an important role to play.

Rote-learning   Box 3.13

... quantities of initial vocabulary can be learned both efficiently and quickly ... by methods such as rote-learning which are not always considered to be respectable. It may be dangerous to underestimate such a capacity. (Carter 1998, p. 193)[17]

What's a car?   Box 3.14

... the child may have a primitive concept of car already, one involving his experiences with the family car, toy cars, cars seen on the street. At some point and for as yet unfathomable reasons, he may hear his father say, Do you want to go in the car?, and conclude that 'car' is the word that refers to his concept, even though he has not been taught the word specifically. (Nelson, 1981, p. 150)[18]

An approach to vocabulary learning that many of us experienced in our classroom-based learning of additional languages was rote-learning. We were typically sent off with a list of words to learn by heart for homework, along with their equivalents in our own language, and were tested on our efforts in the next class. This approach has been much criticised both as theoretically suspect and as bad practice in pedagogical terms. It is clear, however, that repetition forms a normal and natural part of lexical learning. There is '[e]vidence for the existence of a distinct subvocal rehearsal process' (p. 151)[19] when we are dealing with newly encountered words in any language, that is to say we tend to repeat them to ourselves, whether aloud or inaudibly.[19] More generally, verbal memory research indicates that the recall of memorised items is improved by a longer opportunity for rehearsal and that more extensive processing of the items in question tends to increase the durability of the relevant memory codes. Specifically in relation to the second language domain, Nick Ellis found repetition to have a high degree of effectiveness in the learning of second language vocabulary.[20,21]

We discussed earlier how L2 learners make associations between the forms and meanings of words they know and newly encountered items which have some kind of similarity and that the making of such connections is a natural part of the process of acquiring new vocabulary. Another possibility is for learners to deliberately connect new words they come across with words they already know (in their own or another language) to help them retain the new words in question. The use of such 'mnemonic' strategies is something we often do in everyday life in all kinds of areas. For example, if I want to remember the (fictitious!) credit card PIN number 4079, I shall probably associate it with my office number (Room 4079).

Another mnemonic strategy is the so-called 'Keyword Technique', which involves the learner in constructing a mental image which links the newly encountered word with a word which is already known (compare the earlier discussion of the effects of imaging and visualisation on verbal recall). Paul Nation exemplifies the Keyword Technique through an Indonesian learner of English trying to learn the English word *parrot*.[22]

> First, the learner thinks of an Indonesian word that sounds like *parrot* or like a part of *parrot* – for example, the Indonesian word *parit*, which means 'a ditch'. This is the keyword. Second the learner imagines a parrot lying in a ditch! The more striking and unusual the image, the more effective it is. (p. 166)[22]

This sounds fairly outlandish, but it works! The consensus among researchers[23,24] is that the technique is effective across a range of populations and across a range of vocabulary item types, and that it yields good results across different methods of presentation and test-types.

Possible arguments against focusing on individual words in the above manner might be that there is something 'against nature', something 'ecologically invalid' about treating words in isolation from context, and that it fails to prepare learners for dealing with words in connected discourse and text. On the other hand, as we have seen, a prominent aspect of the way in which caregivers interact with young children in many cultures is the phenomenon of ostensive definition; also language learners naturally rehearse individual new items. In any case, given that at least some atomistic techniques are very effective in promoting the retention of new vocabulary, the above argument would carry weight only if the proposal was to deploy such techniques *exclusively*.

Making images   Box 3.15

Go back to the 10 Italian words and see if you can make up images for each one, as Nation suggests.
Was this easy to do?
Would it help you to use them in conversation?

Summary   Box 3.16

- Lexical acquisition is often polarised by researchers into atomistic word-by-word learning and learning from context.
- One technique is rote-learning where words are learnt by ear.
- Another is mnemonic strategies for remembering words by forming mental and verbal associations with them.

Words in context Box 3.17

Try to work out the meaning of the obscure English words in italics from the context. Answers are on p. 51, Box 3.21.

- Imported zebra mussels clog Northeastern waterways, the Korean *hantavirus* invades Baltimore, and Asian mudfish waddle down Florida's roads.
- The year started with the unexpected collapse of a *wichert* cottage in Harwell.
- *Stepovers* are often planted at the front of a border to form an attractive low edging.
- Sages ... Come from the holy fire, perne in a *gyre*, and be the singing masters of my soul.
- It was peels at 8-to-8 in the 10th head as the skip stepped up to the *crampit* to deliver his iron.

Do you think this is the same way that you learn words in a new language?

Learning words from context

Learning words does not have to proceed on an item-by-item basis; nor does it have to involve conscious memorisation at all. It can happen 'through exposure when one's attention is focused on the use of language, rather than on learning' (p. 116).[25] Such learning is possible because of context. Research has shown learners are quite adept at exploiting such help as is provided by context when dealing with unfamiliar second language words, and, in more general terms, has shown a large role for context in lexical processing at every turn of the way. The point of contention is the extent to which working out the meaning and function of words from context of itself has an effect on the retention of vocabulary.

The general argument in favour of the notion that we can acquire second language vocabulary without having to devote special learning or receive special teaching in respect of each item, as put by Evelyn Hatch and Cheryl Brown[26] or by William Nagy[27], is essentially identical to that deployed by Katherine Nelson in relation to first language vocabulary acquisition, namely that the amount of vocabulary we assimilate far exceeds any reasonable assessment of the capacity of special learning or teaching. Nelson's view is that this kind of special attention is almost certainly less important than the mapping from concept to form brought about by meaningful interaction in situations that the learner has already charted in conceptual terms.[18] This can be called incidental vocabulary learning in that it occurs as part of other activities.

Checking learning Box 3.18

How many of the 10 Italian words you looked at earlier can you remember? What does *pigro* mean? What's the Italian for *ring*?

How many of the five 'new' English words you looked at can you remember? What's a *stepover*? Where do you stand to deliver the stone in curling?

Does this show you learn better when you try to learn words deliberately or when you meet them in context without explanation?

A particular view of incidental vocabulary learning was taken by Stephen Krashen, who claimed that new words can be 'picked up' just from reading and from entirely concentrating on the message and the meaning of the texts in question.[28] Studies carried out by Krashen and his collaborators show that the mere reading of a second language text in this way can indeed yield gains in vocabulary – as revealed by surprise vocabulary tests.[29,30] Criticisms of this kind of research have revolved largely around the fact that very small numbers of words seemed to be acquired in this manner and that, in the absence of follow-up tests, it was unclear how long such gains in vocabulary knowledge as were achieved actually lasted.

In SLA research incidental vocabulary learning has been widely written about and discussed on the basis of Krashen's interpretation as simply 'picking up' words in casual encounters, without focused effort being involved. There is, however, a different interpretation of incidental learning, closer to its definition in experimental psychology. In psychology the distinction between incidental and intentional learning has to do with whether or not subjects in an experiment are told in advance that they will be tested on retention. If they are not explicitly encouraged to memorise material, no matter what kinds of focusing experience and operations the experimental task involves, any items retained are regarded as having been acquired incidentally.

An important reference point in relation to this more 'psychological' interpretation of incidental vocabulary learning is the work of two Dutch researchers, Caroline Schouten-van Parreren and Jan Hulstijn. Schouten-van Parreren claims that inferring meaning from context in L2 reading results in better lexical retention than having words and their meanings presented in an isolated manner.[31,32] One person remembered the word *dusk* from a story for instance because she remembered the context of dusk falling on a salt plain used in the story. Schouten-van Parreren contends that new words are more likely to be retained when learners have expended mental effort in relating the items in question to surrounding material and to already existing knowledge. She recommended a three-phase action-sequence:

(1) guessing the meaning of the unknown word;
(2) checking the guess (for example, in a dictionary); and then
(3) focusing on the form of the word, analysing it in relation to other words known.

This action-sequence does not involve trying to memorise the target word, but it does involve paying a good deal of attention to it.

Schouten-van Parreren's research involved the close, detailed scrutiny of L2 learners going about the process of dealing with unfamiliar vocabulary in texts. Hulstijn, for his part, has taken a much more quantitative approach, but his results broadly support Schouten-van Parreren's position, leading him to the following broad conclusions[33,34]:

(1) words are acquired from context in the normal course of reading, although the number of words acquired from any given context on any given occasion is likely to be rather limited;

(2)   the relevance of an unknown word to the informational needs of the learner is a significant factor in relation to the amount of attention the learner gives to that word;

(3)   making an effort to derive the meaning of unknown words from contextual and formal clues improves the chances of such words being retained.

The research outlined above is all concerned with learning vocabulary from reading, and, indeed, most of incidental vocabulary learning research has had a reading orientation. There have, however, been some studies which have shown incidental learning based on oral-aural input. One such study is Lise Duquette's investigation of L2 learners' context-based interaction with audio and video input, which records significant vocabulary gains from both input types.[35] Another contribution is the research of Rod Ellis and his colleagues showing incidental lexical learning from classroom oral interaction.[36,37] Other work has involved, for example, multimedia-supported listening comprehension[38]: visual and auditory aids that the students could call upon while reading text helped their vocabulary acquisition.

Discussion of the development of second language lexical proficiency over time has provided an interesting argument in favour of the idea that context-based vocabulary acquisition may be more effective in terms of fostering second language lexical knowledge which is not dependent on first language lexical competence. A range of evidence suggests that when second language words are first encountered they begin by being associated with first language forms, go on to become associated with first language meanings, and finally evolve autonomous second language form-meaning connections. These three types of organisation are familiar from the categorisation of bilinguals into subordinate, compound and co-ordinate, based on Weinreich,[39] which is outlined in Topic 1. Nan Jiang has suggested that atomistic vocabulary-learning techniques like the Keyword Technique which reinforce L2-L1 links may delay the development of an autonomous L2 lexicon, whereas the context-based approach encourages the inference of genuinely L2 meanings.[40,41] On the other hand, however, as Jiang concedes, many questions concerning incidental vocabulary learning remain unanswered, and before pronouncing on this issue finally we shall need to know a good deal much more about the relevant psycholinguistic processes and their consequences in terms of how words are organised and represented under different conditions.

Uses of context

Box 3.19

The first ['atomistic'] approach does not emphasize the provision of contextualized input ... and is more likely to encourage the learner's tendency to rely on L1. The second approach encourages meaning inference and attempts to minimize the reliance on L1. Given the relation ... between input and reliance on L1 on one side and lexical representation and development on the other, the second [context-based] approach seems to provide better conditions for the development of lexical competence. (Jiang, 2000, p. 70)[40]

But not all contexts are equally rich in terms of the information they make available in respect of unfamiliar words, with the result that the meanings derived are not always very specific. Clearly, the word-meanings we acquire from context are no more precise than the contextual information provided by that context as cues for meaning. For example, let us say I am a learner of French in France and that I see one of my French friends limping towards me in obvious pain. *Qu'est-ce qu'il y a?* ('What's the matter?'), I may ask. The response I may get is *J'ai un problème avec ma cheville*. Now, if I do not know the word *cheville*, neither the linguistic context 'I have a problem with my ...' nor the general context will tell me that *cheville* means 'ankle'. 'Knee', 'hip', even 'leg' would fit the context equally well.

Some concluding remarks

The mental lexicon, whether in the first language or in additional languages, involves a great deal more than individual word forms and their basic meanings, and the learning of vocabulary has to be seen as a much richer, more multidimensional and more interesting activity than it was traditionally considered to be.

Lexical acquisition may be facilitated by biologically endowed mechanisms relating to specific aspects of the process. Even if this is the case, however, universal innate language-acquiring can only take the process so far. At the level of particular forms and their association with particular concept configurations, the person coming to grips with a language, first or second, actually has to *learn*.

Both first language and second language vocabulary acquisition proceed in a context of input tuning of various kinds and are characterised by 'special teaching' in the form of ostensive definitions – reflecting an intuition on the part of their interlocutors that learners require constant attentiveness to their comprehension problems, continual support and a generous supply of explicit explanations. The importance of image in lexical acquisition suggests that learners could be helped by encouraging them to use images and imaging techniques to come to grips with new items. The gains yielded by encountering new words in meaningful environments and situations appropriate to learners' needs imply that vocabulary learning benefits from as rich and interesting input and interaction as possible.

The defining difference between first language and second language lexical acquisition is that in the latter case the process inevitably interacts with the already existing lexical knowledge of the first language. In many respects such interaction may actually assist the learner. In any case, as second language proficiency increases, the dependency of second language lexical knowledge on the first language lexical knowledge diminishes and the autonomy of the second language lexical knowledge increases.

Finally, vocabulary learning in an additional language has both an atomistic and a context-based dimension. Both dimensions clearly have a significant role to play in the process. It is interesting to note that across a wide variety of teaching methodologies, based on widely different theoretical foundations, the value of both atomistic and context-based approaches has consistently been implicitly assumed by course designers.

Postscript   Box 3.20

Polonius: What do you read, my lord?

Hamlet: Words, words, words.

Shakespeare, *Hamlet,* Act 2 Scene 2

In the beginning was the Word, and the Word was with God, and the Word was God.
King James Bible, John, 1.1

Words are the daughters of earth, and things are the sons of Heaven.
Dr Johnson

In the light of the complexity of vocabulary seen in this chapter, do you think these are good summaries?

Answers to 'Words in context': Box 3.17, p. 47   Box 3.21

A *hantavirus* is a type of single-stranded RNA virus.
Wichert is chalk mud mixed with straw.
Stepovers are low apple trees.
A *gyre* is a circling turn.
A *crampit* is a footboard for a curling player.
For a fuller test go to: http://homepage.ntlworld.com/vivian.c/Words/WordTests/TESTcontext.htm

Further reading

Some useful book-length general treatments of second language vocabulary learning include:

Nation, I.S.P. (2001) *Learning Vocabulary in Another Language.* Cambridge: Cambridge University Press.

Pavičić Takač, V. (2008) *Vocabulary Learning Strategies and Foreign Language Acquisition.* Clevedon: Multilingual Matters.

Qing Ma (2009) *Second Language Vocabulary Acquisition.* Bern: Peter Lang.

The following books have mainly a classroom and/or vocabulary testing orientation:

Kerste, S. (2010) *The Mental Lexicon and Vocabulary Learning: Implications for the Foreign Language Classroom.* Tübingen: Narr Francke Attempto.

Meara, P. (2009) *Connected Words: Word Associations and Second Language Vocabulary Acquisition.* Amsterdam: John Benjamins.

Milton, J. (2009) *Measuring Second Language Vocabulary Acquisition.* Bristol: Multilingual Matters.

Below are three collections of material which deal with a wide array of lexical topics and are well worth exploring

Bogaards, P. and Laufer, B. (eds) (2004) *Vocabulary in a Second Language: Selection, Acquisition, and Testing.* Amsterdam: John Benjamins.

Chacón-Beltrán, R., Abello-Contesse, C. and Torreblanca-López, M. (eds) (2010) *Insights into Non-native Vocabulary Teaching and Learning.* Bristol: Multilingual Matters.

Lengyel, Z. and Navracsics. J. (eds) (2007) *Second Language Lexical Processes: Applied Linguistic and Psycholinguistic Processes.* Clevedon: Multilingual Matters.

For those readers who are interested in the issues surrounding incidental and intentional vocabulary learning, an authoritative review is:

Hulstijn, J.H. (2003) Incidental and intentional learning. In C.J. Doughty and M.H. Long (eds) (2003) *The Handbook of Second Language Acquisition.* Oxford: Blackwell, 349–381.

Also well worth looking at in this connection – though a quarter of a century old – is:

Drum, P.A. and Konopak, B.C. (1987) Learning word meanings from written context. In M.G. McKeown and M.E. Curtis (eds) (1987) *The Nature of Vocabulary Acquisition.* Hillsdale, NJ: Lawrence Erlbaum, 73–87.

References

1. Hurford, J. (1994) *Grammar: A Student's Guide.* Cambridge: Cambridge University Press.

2. Sapir, E. (1921) *Language: An Introduction to the Study of Speech.* New York: Harcourt Brace & World.

3. *Oxford English Dictionary* (2009) Oxford: Oxford University Press. Online at: http://www.oed.com/

4. Clark, E.V. and Andersen, E.S. (1979) Spontaneous repairs: Awareness in the process of acquiring language. *Papers and Reports on Child Language Development* 16 (distributed by ERIC Clearinghouse).

5. Lehr, F., Osborn, O.J. and Hiebert, E.H. (2004) *A Focus on Vocabulary.* Honolulu: Pacific Resources for Education and Learning.

6. Chomsky, N. (2000) *New Horizons in the Study of Language and Mind.* Cambridge: Cambridge University Press.

7. Clark, E.V. (2009) *First Language Acquisition,* 2nd edition. Cambridge: Cambridge University Press.

8. Pinker, S. (1994) *The Language Instinct: How the Mind Creates Language.* New York, NY: Harper.

9. Swan, M. (1997) The influence of the mother tongue on second language vocabulary acquisition and use. In N. Schmitt and M. McCarthy (eds) (1997) *Vocabulary: Description, Acquisition and Pedagogy*. Cambridge: Cambridge University Press, 156–180.

10. Gass, S.M. and Selinker, L. (2008) *Second Language Acquisition: An Introductory Course*, 2nd edition. London: Routledge.

11. Cohen, A. and Aphek, E. (1980) Retention of second-language vocabulary over time: Investigating the role of mnemonic associations. *System* 8 (3), 221–235.

12. Singleton, D. and Ó Laoire, M. (2006) Psychotypology and the 'L2 factor' in cross-lexical interaction: An analysis of English and Irish influence in learner French. In M. Bendtsen, M. Björklund, C. Fant and L. Forsman (eds) (2006) *Språk, Lärande och Utbildning i Sikte*. Vasa: Faculty of Education, Åbo Akademi, 191–205.

13. Ellis, N.C. (1995) Vocabulary acquisition: Psychological perspectives. *The Language Teacher* 19 (2), 12–16.

14. Tomlinson, B. (1996) Helping L2 readers to see. In T. Hickey and J. Williams (eds) (1996) *Language, Education and Society in a Changing World*. Clevedon: IRAAL/Multilingual Matters, 253–262.

15. Danesi, M. (2012) *Italian Now!* 2nd edition. New York: Barrons.

16. Carter, R. (1998) *Vocabulary: Applied Linguistic Perspectives*. London: Routledge.

17. Nelson, K. (1981) Acquisition of words by first-language learners. In H. Winitz (ed.) (1981) *Native Language and Foreign Language Acquisition*. New York: The New York Academy of Sciences, 148–159.

18. Byrne, J.H. (2008) *Concise Learning and Memory: The Editor's Selection*. New York: Academic Press.

19. Ellis, N.C. and Beaton, A. (1993) Factors affecting the learning of foreign language vocabulary: Imagery keyword mediators and phonological short-term memory. *Quarterly Journal of Experimental Psychology: Human Experimental Psychology* 46A (3), 533–558.

20. Ellis, N.C. and Beaton, A. (1995) Psycholinguistic determinants of foreign language vocabulary learning. In B. Harley (ed.) (1995) *Lexical Issues in Language Learning*. Amsterdam: Language Learning/John Benjamins, 107–165.

21. Nation, P. (1990) *Teaching and Learning Vocabulary*. Boston, MA: Heinle & Heinle.

22. Pressley, M., Levin, J.R. and McDaniel, M.A. (1987) Remembering versus inferring what a word means: Mnemonic and contextual approaches. In M.G. McKeown and M.E. Curtis (eds) (1987) *The Nature of Vocabulary Acquisition*. Hillsdale, NJ: Lawrence Erlbaum, 107–128.

23. Rodriguez, M. and Sadoski, M. (2000) Effects of rote, context, keyword and context/keyword methods of retention of vocabulary in EFL classrooms. *Language Learning* 50 (2), 385–412.

24. Schmitt, N. (2000) *Vocabulary in Language Teaching*. Cambridge: Cambridge University Press.

25. Hatch, E. and Brown, C. (1995) *Vocabulary, Semantics and Language Education*. Cambridge: Cambridge University Press.

26. Nagy, W. (1997) On the role of context in first- and second-language vocabulary learning. In N. Schmitt and M. McCarthy (eds) (1997) *Vocabulary: Description, Acquisition and Pedagogy.* Cambridge: Cambridge University Press, 64–83.

27. Krashen, S. (1989) We acquire vocabulary and spelling by reading: Additional evidence for the input hypothesis. *Modern Language Journal* 73 (4), 440–464.

28. Pitts, M., White, H. and Krashen, S. (1989) Acquiring second language vocabulary through reading: A replication of the Clockwork Orange study using second language acquirers. *Reading in a Foreign Language* 5 (2), 271–275.

29. Dupuy, B. and Krashen, S. (1993) Incidental vocabulary acquisition in French as a second language. *Applied Language Learning* 4 (1), 55–63.

30. Schouten-van Parreren, C. (1989) Vocabulary learning through reading: Which conditions should be met when presenting words in texts? *AILA Review* 6, 75–85.

31. Schouten-van Parreren, C. (1992) Individual differences in vocabulary acquisition: A qualitative experiment in the first phase of secondary education. In P. Arnaud and H. Béjoint (eds) (1992) *Vocabulary and Applied Linguistics.* Houndmills: Macmillan, 94–101.

32. Hulstijn, J. (1992) Retention of inferred and given word meanings: Experiments in incidental vocabulary learning. In P. Arnaud and H. Béjoint (eds) (1992) *Vocabulary and Applied Linguistics.* Houndmills: Macmillan, 113–125.

33. Hulstijn, J. (1993–1994) L'acquisition incidente du lexique en cours de la lecture: ses avantages et ses limites. *Acquisition et interaction en Langue Étrangère* 3, 77–96.

34. Duquette, L. (1993) *L'étude de l'apprentissage du vocabulaire en contexte par l'écoute d'un dialogue scénarisé en français langue seconde.* Quebec: Université Laval, Centre International de Recherche en Aménagement Linguistique.

35. Ellis, R., Tanaka, Y. and Yamazaki, A. (1994) Classroom interaction, comprehension, and the acquisition of L2 word meanings. *Language Learning* 44 (3), 449–491.

36. Ellis, R. and Fotos, S. (1999) *Learning a Second Language through Interaction.* Amsterdam: John Benjamins.

37. Jones, L.C. (2003) Supporting listening comprehension and vocabulary acquisition with multimedia annotations: The students' voice. *CALICO Journal* 21 (1), 41–65.

38. Weinreich, U. (1953) *Languages in Contact.* The Hague: Mouton.

39. Jiang, N. (2000) Lexical development and representation in a second language. *Applied Linguistics* 21 (1), 47–77.

40. Jiang, N. (2004) Semantic transfer and its implications for vocabulary teaching in a second language. *The Modern Language Journal* 88 (3), 416–432.

4

How Important is Grammar in Acquiring and Using a Second Language?

Vivian Cook

After unfortunate experiences at school with lessons about the three kinds of conditional clause or the profound differences between *must* and *have to*, many people are worried that any discussion of grammar is bound to be both difficult to understand and extremely boring. Yet grammar is an everyday tool that people use all the time without being aware of it. For grammar is just the way we put sentences together to communicate what we want to say, almost as important as breathing and just as unobtrusive.

Starter: What is grammar? Box 4.1

What do you think grammar actually *is*?

- Rules for behaviour that you shouldn't break?
- Mental processes for structuring language?
- Sets of patterns for arranging words in sentences?

Can you give an example of a grammatical rule? Does it work?

How important do you think grammar is in learning and teaching a second language?

At one level, grammar is the elaborate technical description found in grammar books, for English say the 1204 pages of the *Longman Grammar of Spoken and Written English*.[1] These large-scale grammars describe the ideal version of the whole language and are valuable resources for finding out everything that could possibly be said in English. At another level, grammar refers to the grammatical resources an individual speaker of a language has in their mind – the ability to put sentences together to convey a meaning and the ability to squeeze the meaning out of them. You can't speak or understand any sentence fully without grasping its grammatical structure. Grammar is a practical necessity for communicating in a language and underlies everything we say and comprehend.

Box 4.2 illustrates some basic grammatical differences between languages, starting from the English sentence *The plumber mended the broken pipes.* Knowing and using a language means knowing how to put together sentences according to its grammar.

Some basic grammar differences between languages Box 4.2

English: The plumber mended the broken pipes.

Italian:	L'idraulico	aggiustò	i	tubi	rotti.
	(the plumber	mended	the	pipes	broken)

Arabic:	Aslaha	alsabbaku	alanabeeba	almaksorata.
	(mended	the plumber	the pipes	broken)

Arabic script (right to left): أصلح السباك الأنابيب المكسورة

Chinese:	Shuinuangong ba	duanlie	guandao	xiuhao	le.
	(plumber	broken	pipes	mend	past)

Chinese script: 水暖工把断裂管道修好了

An important resource for grammar is *word order*. Grammar takes advantage of the fact that words have to come one after the other by making this order of words itself have meaning, even if a few languages such as Hungarian and Turkish have much freer word orders. In languages like English the word order of a sentence communicates the basic relationship of words in the sentence – essentially who is doing what to whom. Unless you understand what the order conveys, you will have little idea of what is going on.

In English the subject noun phrase comes before the verb phrase which in turn comes before the object noun phrase: *The plumber* (subject) *mended* (verb) *the broken pipes* (object). In Arabic, however, the verb *Aslaha* ('mended') comes before the subject *alsabbaku* ('the plumber'). In the Chinese sentence, both the subject *shuinuangong* ('plumber') and the object *duanlie guandao* ('broken pipes') come before the verb *xiuhao* ('mend') (but only in sentences with the particle *ba*). English, Chinese and Arabic use very different orders to convey essentially the same meaning. The word order within phrases is also important. In English and Chinese, the adjective comes before the noun, *broken pipes* and *duanlie guandao*. But in Italian and Arabic the adjective comes after the noun, *tubi rotti* and *alanabeeba almaksorata* ('pipes broken').

A second major resource for grammar is *changing the form of words*. This can be done through inflections on the end of the word, as with the past tense inflection *-ed* in English *mended* or the past tense inflection *-ò* in Italian *aggiustò*. Or it can be done by changing the vowels within the verb as in the Arabic *aslaha,* similar to the vowel changes a few English irregular verbs like *bite/bit* or *fly/flew*. Such changes in the form of words can be used to express ideas of tense and time as in *mends/mended*, the roles of subject and object in the sentence *he/him*, and many other concepts.

A major grammatical force in many languages is 'agreement', which links different parts of the sentence together; nouns, adjectives or articles agree with each other in terms of gender, number or other grammatical properties. In Italian and Arabic the verb has different endings to agree in singular or plural number with the subject; in Italian the verb *aggiustò* ('mend') has a singular inflection to agree with the singular subject *L'idraulic* ('the plumber'). Chinese has no agreement as words do not change their form. English has a small amount of number agreement, chiefly in the present tense *they like/he likes* where subject and verb agree.

A third resource is *grammatical systems*: according to Michael Halliday, 'the grammar is seen as a network of interrelated meaningful choices'.[2] Articles, sometimes known as determiners, form one such system. English has three articles, *the/a(n)/Ø* (a sign for zero article, i.e. no article at all), as in *the man/a man/Ø man/Ø men*. Italian articles agree with nouns for number and gender: *i tubi* ('the pipes', masculine plural), *le mani* ('the hands', feminine plural). Arabic has a definite article *al*, used with nouns – *alsabbaku* ('the plumber') – and with adjectives – *almaksorata* ('broken'). Many languages, however, do not have articles, like Chinese. Articles are often used to express whether specific things are meant – *the/a teacher* – or things in general – *Ø truth* – and whether things have already been mentioned – *an elephant* – or are being mentioned for the first time – *the elephant*. A grammatical system consists of a choice between meaningful grammatical options. The English article system has a choice of three articles in the singular *the/a/Ø* and two in the plural *the/Ø*, each linked to particular meanings, to be elaborated below.

Summary: Some aspects of grammar   Box 4.3

- *word order*, particularly the order of subject (S), verb (V) and object (O), e.g. SVO (English), SOV (German), VSO (Arabic);
- *inflections*, such as possessive 's, and past tense tense *-ed*. Often the inflections of different words in the sentence 'agree' to show number (*the boy is here/the boys are here*) or gender;
- *grammatical systems*, such as the article system *a/the/Ø*, where one item of the set is chosen to express a particular meaning, seen in greater detail in Box 4.12.

Learning the grammar of a second language

The basics of word order, inflection and grammatical system underpin any use of language. In our first language, these have been acquired over many years of infancy, along with all the other things that children learn. We take them for granted and probably assume that that is just the way language is – until we come up against the kinds of difference seen in Box 4.2.

Grammar is just as important in a second language: we would not do very well in conversation in a second language if we didn't know its basic word order, its common inflections (or the lack of them) and its system of articles. An English speaker learning Chinese has to learn how to express past tense through a particle *le* rather than an inflection *-ed*; a Chinese person learning Italian has to learn to put adjectives after nouns – *tubi rotti*. And so on for all the myriad grammatical differences between languages. Almost everything we take for granted about putting sentences together in our first language can be wrong in a second language, except for the lucky chance that the new language shares the same grammatical features as the old.

The grammar that L2 learners acquire in a second language can't be the same as the grammar of a monolingual native speaker, partly because of the first language grammar they already possess, partly because of the different ways and circumstances in which a second language is acquired and used. It is therefore unrealistic to measure the grammar of L2 users against that of monolingual native speakers; they are bound to be different. But difference does not mean deficiency. An L2 grammar has to do different things from an L1 grammar and forms part of a larger overall system.

A commonsense belief is that learning another language involves learning bits of the native grammar and gradually putting them together into a whole system: first the learner acquires the present tense, then the present continuous, and so on, until all the English tenses have been mastered, rather like a jigsaw puzzle in which all the bits gradually build up into a picture which is only complete when the last bit is in place. But grammar doesn't work like that. A grammar hangs together as a whole, a complex system of word order, inflections and grammatical systems involved in every sentence; the shapes of the bits of the jigsaw change as more are added and they make a complete picture at each stage.

L2 learners might use some version of the present tense – *She laugh* – in the overall grammatical system they possess; it has a limited meaning for them within their grammar of the moment, however simple that may be. Then they expand the system as they gain the present continuous; you only know part of the meaning of present tense – *She laughs* – if you don't know how it contrasts with present continuous tense – *She's laughing* – and later on, say, with past tense – *She laughed* – present perfect tense – *She has laughed* – and all the other possibilities in English. The meaning of the jigsaw piece called present tense does not stay the same but develops as the learner progresses not only in contrast with the other tenses that are learnt but also to include such subtleties as the future meaning, *My train leaves at six*, 'eternal truths', *The sun sets in the west*, and its compulsory use with 'personal' verbs – in standard British English you cannot say *I am knowing this* or *I am believing this*, even if these occur in other varieties.

In the early 1960s people researching children's language acquisition realised that children have mental grammars of their own at each stage of language development – the 'independent grammar assumption'.[3] Children don't so much pick up bits of adult grammar as invent a grammar system of their own. Hence the weirdness to us of such ordinary two-word children's sentences as *More up*, *Slug coming* and *Help jelly*, natural as they seem to the children. Jerome Bruner claimed that the extraordinary aspect of language acquisition was how well adults coped with children's language, rather than how easily the children acquired language.[4]

This idea of the learner's independent grammar was taken up by SLA researchers under the name of 'interlanguage' – a name for the learner's system as a grammar in its own right rather than as a defective version of the target language.[5]

Figure 4.1 shows how L2 learners create an interlanguage grammar of their own out of the first language they already know, the fragments of the second language they encounter, and their other experiences such as teaching, social encounters and so on. The inescapable difference from L1 children is the presence of the first language in their minds. Their exposure to the second language and their other influences may also differ considerably from the young child's, depending on their circumstances. Much language teaching has, however, endeavoured precisely to make the conditions of learning as similar to the child's as possible, as we see in Topic 7, whether the visual links of the audio-visual method between pictures and words or the conversational interaction of communicative teaching where students have to communicate to each other in the classroom.

A clear interlanguage grammar was seen in the basic L2 grammar discovered by Wolfgang Klein and Clive Perdue,[6] shown in Box 4.4. This was based on the sentences of adult speakers of six languages, including Finnish and Punjabi, using five second languages, including Dutch and Swedish. The L2 users' sentences are not much like those of a native speaker. The German sentence *Mädchen nehme Brot* lacks the German

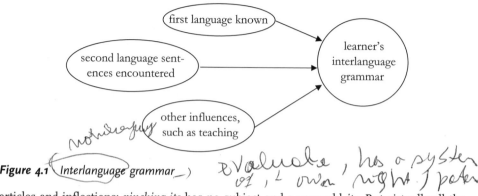

Figure 4.1 (Interlanguage grammar)

[handwritten annotations: "notnebrofnly", "evaluate, has a system of, 1 own, right] poter"]

articles and inflections; *pinching its* has no subject and a very odd *its*. But virtually all the L2 users' sentences could be covered by the simple rules of the basic L2 grammar given in Box 4.4: *either* a sentence starts with a noun followed by a verb or *be*, *or* the noun and verb are followed by another noun or adjective, *or* the sentence consists of a verb, sometimes followed by a noun. That's it – no need for a 1204-page grammar.

A basic interlanguage grammar for any language Box 4.4

A sentence may have:

(1) a noun followed by a verb (and sometimes another noun): *Mädchen nehme Brot* ('girl take bread');

(2) a noun followed by a form of *be* and another noun or an adjective: *it's bread*;

(3) a verb followed by a noun phrase: *pinching its*.[6]

This basic three-rule grammar was shared by L2 users from different backgrounds with different first languages. The peculiarities of the first and second language didn't make much difference: almost all of them created the same rules, which sometimes resembled the native speaker grammar, sometimes not. L2 learners are creating a mental interlanguage grammar of their own, in the same way as L1 children.

So how important is the first language the L2 learner already knows? Look at the collection of L2 student sentences in Box 4.5 and see if you can guess which first language each student speaks.

Some sentences from L2 students Box 4.5

(1) ... we have many book about him;

(2) ... one of the most important things in the American social relationship is a punctuality;

(3) I have experienced myself many culture shocks;

(4) They proud of it very much;

(5) Other problem not commun now is the tenant, who wants finish with the problem shoot him or going to the war and is xxxxx his own gun;

(6) I just eight months before here;

(7) ... Because then have you to speak in every situation (in this language,);

(8) The government try to bring the most advantage things to develope the nation.

Answers in Box 4.17 on p. 70

I dialect = the way one speaks.

Most people only get a small proportion of these right. The main reason is the similar grammars that L2 learners invent for themselves. The lack of inflections, *book* (no. 1), the odd articles, *a punctuality* (2), the missing verbs, (6) *I just eight months before here*, and the odd word order, (4) *They proud of it very much*, all occur in many L2 learners of English, not just the speakers of a single first language. Perhaps the word order in (3) strikes one as like French, *I have experienced myself many culture shocks*, with that in (7) like German, *Because then have you to speak*. While no one denies the effects of the first language on the second language, researchers have often been surprised by how much learners with different first languages actually have in common.

Nevertheless the first language is part of the whole language system in the learner's mind and its grammar is bound to affect the sentences the learner produces in the second language. The traditional name for this effect was 'transfer' and it was seen as a negative force that interfered with the acquisition of the second language. For instance a German learner of English might transfer the structure of the German sentence *Gestern kam er* to English and say *Yesterday came he*. Or a Spanish learner of English might transfer the subject-less structure of *Son las tres* to English to get *Is three o'clock*.

This leads in to a famous grammatical point in Chomsky's Universal Grammar, called the pro-drop parameter, summarised in Box 4.6. One way of expressing the cross-linguistic variation between languages is as a set of parameters which are given different values in each language, rather like a set of light switches for a large room, each of which can be set to on or off. So the pro-drop parameter has two values: subjects are set either as compulsory or as optional in any human language. In so-called non-pro-drop languages like English and German, the sentence has to have a subject even if it's only a pronoun; *I'm from Rome* or *It's raining*. In pro-drop languages like Japanese or Italian, the sentence doesn't necessarily have to have a subject, *Sono di Roma* ('am from Rome'), or *Piove* ('raining'). Transferring the Italian pro-drop value for the parameter to English yields L2 learner sentences like *Am from Rome* and *Is raining*.

Pro-drop and non-pro-drop languages		Box 4.6
Pro-drop languages Allow subject-less sentences like Italian *Pluve* ('rains')		**Non-pro-drop languages** Do not allow subject-less sentences
Italian Chinese Arabic Greek Portuguese Spanish Hebrew Japanese Etc.		German French English Dutch

Clearly the interlanguage grammar the learners create draws in part on their first languages. Only recently has it become apparent that the second language also affects the first language that the person already knows. To take pro-drop as an example once again, the value for the new language has an effect on the old. An Italian learning English has to switch from a grammar with a pro-drop setting to one with a non-pro-drop setting. If they carry this back to Italian, they will start overlarding their sentences with subjects and say *Io*

Transfert: is when one make a mistake in transfer from L₁ to L₂.

61

sono di Roma with a subject *io* ('I'), comparatively rare in Italian. While sentences with subject pronouns do occur in pro-drop languages, they usually carry some special emphasis, and so sound rather odd if they are used constantly. Greek students in England have said that, when they go home, their parents tell them off because their Greek sounds English, i.e. they have too many subjects. This may of course be an asset; there is a legendary coterie of Tokyo housewives who deliberately use extra subjects in Japanese sentences to sound cosmopolitan.

There are many other examples of the effects of the second language on the first. Children learning Cherokee as a second language are less likely to coin past tense forms such as *taked* and *comed* in their L1 English than English-speaking children without Cherokee.[7] A Finnish L2 user of English rejected Finnish sentences that were perfectly acceptable because they did not follow the English word order.[8]

This is called 'reverse transfer' as it goes backwards from the second language to the first. Your L1 grammar is no longer quite the same if you speak another language. I often use a construction in English, *What's that for a book?*, which I can only attribute to the Swiss-German I was exposed to as a child. Once the language system of a multilingual is treated as a whole, interconnections occur between all the languages a multilingual possesses. So people have also talked of 'lateral transfer' which goes between two of the speaker's non-native languages, say from the second to the third, and of 'bidirectional transfer' in which the two languages influence each other mutually.[9]

Summary: The links between the two languages ('transfer' or 'cross-linguistic influence')

Box 4.7

L1 > L2   – the first language influences some aspect of the second.
L2 > L1   – the second language influences some aspect of the first.
L1 <> L2 – the first and second languages both influence each other.
L2 > L3   – the second language influences the third language.

The term 'transfer' is now less used because it suggests taking something and putting it somewhere else – take the German article *das* and pop it into English and hope it works: there is after all a TV commercial in England for Volkswagen that proclaims *Das Auto*. What is happening is more like a continuous connection between languages that get entwined into a complex network – combining aspects of the German article system with the L2 system emerging from the sentences heard. Hence the more current term is 'cross-linguistic influence', a continuing relationship between the languages.[9] The study of cross-linguistic influence also extends to what happens when people lose their first or second languages, called 'attrition', an exciting modern area of SLA research.[10]

Opinions on grammar

Box 4.8

Which of these do you agree with?

• Grammar is unimportant.	☐ Yes	☐ No	☐ Don't know
• Grammar is just logical thinking.	☐ Yes	☐ No	☐ Don't know
• Grammatical mistakes are very serious.	☐ Yes	☐ No	☐ Don't know
• Language teachers shouldn't explain grammar.	☐ Yes	☐ No	☐ Don't know

---

Three areas of grammar

Let us take three examples from different areas of L2 grammar. Of course these are only a sample of the many areas of grammar that have been researched and of the diverse approaches used to analyse them.

Grammatical morphemes

Some of the earliest research on SLA grammar looked at how L2 learners acquire the grammatical inflections and function words of English, grouped together as 'grammatical morphemes'. The psychologist Roger Brown[11] had observed that young English children acquiring their first language typically leave these out of the sentences; a two-year-old is more likely to say *Mummy go shop* than *Mummy is going to the shops*. He established that children start introducing these forms into their speech in a particular sequence over time.

Heidi Dulay and Marina Burt adapted this methodology to SLA research by scoring the proportion of particular grammatical morphemes missing from Spanish-speaking children's description of pictures in English, finding the following order:[12]

1	2	3	4	5	6	7
the/a	*-ing*	plural *-s*	regular past *-ed*	irregular past	possessive *'s*	3rd person *-s*

Figure 4.2 *Dulay & Burt[12] difficulty order for English grammatical morphemes*

The most used grammatical morpheme was the articles *the/a, a cake;* the second was the present continuous ending *-ing, cooking;* then in order came the plural *-s, cakes,* the regular past inflection *-ed, cooked,* and the irregular past tense, *ate;* the least used items were the possessive *-s, John's cake* and the 3rd person singular *-s* of the verb, *cooks the cake.* This order of difficulty seems to correspond with how the grammar develops chronologically. As learners progress, the sentence gets fleshed out with more inflections and grammatical words, i.e. gains grammatical structure.

Similar orders were found for the appearance of these elements in learners' sentences from speakers from many different first languages and in many different circumstances, say attending a language class or not. One study looked at how Bengali-speaking primary school children in the East End of London acquired verbal inflections.[13] The present continuous *-ing* came chronologically first but the irregular past tenses like *went* followed rather than preceded the regular past form *-ed.*

The conclusion is that the acquisition of these elements occurs in definite stages, even if the details vary from one piece of research to another. To generalise from this, grammatical elements of a second language are learnt in a similar order, varying only slightly according to their first language or the teaching method they have encountered. This particular point was confirmed time and again in different areas of SLA research, as other chapters in this book show; second language acquisition occurs in stages that are common to many, if not most, learners, whether sounds, grammatical structures, or other areas of language. SLA research more or less takes it for granted that L2 acquisition takes part in a sequence of stages.

Interesting as stages of acquisition may be, they don't say *why* things happen in a particular order – data looking for an explanation. One possibility put forward was that it's the 'natural order',[14] which is really no explanation at all: whatever is is natural; the question is *why* is it natural? The Processability Model proposed by Manfred Pienemann, however, bases the sequence of development upon the learner's increasing mental capacity to process a new language.[15] It claims that learners' stages reflect how their memory expands in the second language over time, namely:

Sequences of second language acquisition   Box 4.9

These are some of the sequences of acquisition of grammar that have been claimed for second language acquisition:

- grammatical morphemes[12]:
     the/a > -ing > pl. -s > reg. past –ed > irreg. past > poss. 's > 3rd pers. -s
- processability[15]:
     fly > will fly > I will fly > I will fly if possible
- negation[16]:
     Kenny no>No finish>That's no good>You have a not fish>You didn't can throw it

---

(1) *using single content words.* At the outset their small memory capacity means that L2 learners are only able to process one word at a time. So they produce utterances consisting of individual content words: *Husband. Fly. Plane. Thursday.*

(2) *adding function words.* As their capacity increases slightly, the learners can start to put function words into the sentence: *Husband. Fly. To Paris. On Thursday.*

(3) *making phrases.* Given more capacity, the learners can now assemble these words into phrases: *My husband. Will fly. To Paris. On Thursday.*

(4) *making sentences.* With still more capacity available, the learners can assemble the different parts into a sentence: *My husband will fly to Paris on Thursday.* This is the point at which they have command of the main structure and word order of the simple sentence.

(5) *adding subordinate clauses.* Finally the learner gains enough capacity to be able to insert subordinate clauses within the sentence: *My husband will fly to Paris on Thursday if the airport is open.*

Each stage shows the learner's increasing capacity to process crucial elements of the sentence.

Word order and processing

As we saw, one way of identifying the subject of an English sentence is to look for the noun or noun phrase that comes first. The subject of *Sherlock Holmes plays the violin* is

Sherlock Holmes because it comes first, before the verb. A theory called the Competition Model has explored different ways of finding the subject as people process the sentence on the wing.[17] This relies on an experimental technique shown in Box 4.10. Try to say which is the subject of each sentence, even if they seem very odd.

Which is the subject of the sentence?   Box 4.10

Underline the subject:

(1)   The dog pats the tree.
(2)   The horse the rock kisses.
(3)   Watches the monkey the pen.
(4)   The pencil smells the giraffe.
(5)   The ball the cat bites.
(6)   Licks the spoon the bear.
(7)   The dogs bites the monkey.
(8)   The cows the cat watches.
(9)   Pats the pigs the giraffe.
(10) The monkeys pats the giraffe.
(11) The bears the turtle pulls.
(12) Greets the pigs the monkey.

In some languages the subject must refer to something that is alive rather than dead. In *Sherlock Holmes plays the violin*, the subject *Sherlock Holmes* is both first and alive. So in *The violin struck Sherlock Holmes on the head*, English speakers would see *the violin* as the subject as it comes first in the sentence although it is not of course animate. In languages like Japanese, however, animacy takes precedence over word order: *Sherlock Holmes* is the subject of the sentence despite not coming first. So for Japanese the subject of sentence (4) *The pencil smells the giraffe* would be the giraffe.

In sentence (10) *The monkeys pats the giraffe*, the singular *the giraffe* agrees with the singular verb *pats*. In some languages like Italian this subject-verb agreement is far more important than word order, making *the giraffe* the subject. So while an odd sentence like (7) *The dogs bites the monkey* would, to an English speaker, still have *the dogs* as the subject, an Italian would feel *the monkey* was the subject, unlikely as the meaning might be: the subject is the noun that agrees in number with the verb.

In short the grammatical function of subject is shown by different cues such as word order, animacy and number agreement. Sometimes these may coincide so that *Sherlock Holmes* is both singular, animate and first in the sentence. The experimental sentences in Box 4.10 split up the cues so that their relative strength can be seen. In any language, one of these cues usually overrides the others, in English word order, in Japanese animacy and in Italian agreement. Processing the sentence means finding the right cue to the subject, which may differ in the first and second language.

The first SLA research into this interpreted it as transfer from the first language to the second. Dutch prefers agreement and sure enough Dutch speakers of English rely more on agreement in English than native English speakers.[18] In Turkish, animacy is most important and so Turkish learners of Dutch over-rely on animacy when using Dutch.[19] It is not just the grammatical structure that is transferred from the first language to the second, it is also the ways in which the sentence is processed in our minds.

More recently this methodology has been applied to reverse transfer – the effects of the second language on the first.[20] Sure enough speakers of Japanese, Greek, Arabic and Spanish who know English are influenced by the English preference for word order when speaking their first language. They no longer choose the subject for quite the same reasons as their monolingual peers who do not speak English.

This area shows clearly the interconnections between the languages in the L2 user's mind. The first and second language grammars do not function independently but are always related. Processing the second language depends partly on the first, processing the first language partly on the second. Whichever language the L2 user is using, whatever other languages the person knows remain present in the system and can never be completely switched off.

Summary: Subject cues in second language acquisition   Box 4.11

(1) Languages differ in the cues for recognising the subject of the sentence by its position, its animacy, its agreement and so on.
(2) The L1 cues may have an effect on the acquisition of the second language.
(3) The L2 cues may have some effect on the first language the person knows.

Articles

Let us turn to the grammatical system of articles. These are used in many languages to convey a range of different meanings, though are completely absent from other languages. The learning of articles in a second language seems a particularly fraught enterprise.

The English articles are a test case. With singular nouns, there are three possibilities: the definite article *the* beer, the indefinite article *a* beer/*an* orange, and the zero article (Ø) *beer*, i.e. no article at all. With plural nouns, there are two possibilities: *the beers* and Ø *beers*.

A crucial aspect of the meaning of articles is countability. When a noun is countable, it can have *a/an* in the singular: *a book* but not Ø *book*; when it is uncountable, the reverse applies: *honesty* but not *an honesty*. We see from the example of *beer* that it is the meaning that is dominant in our minds which is relevant, not the particular noun; one can say both *I'll have a beer* (countable) and *Beer is an alcoholic drink* (uncountable); *a beer* refers to a countable glass or type of beer, not to the uncountable liquid itself referred to by *beer*; countability depends on the aspect of meaning the speaker wishes to convey. The word *some* also acts as part of the article system and can be used with uncountable nouns: *some beer*.

If nouns like *guitar* or *ostrich* used countably refer to something believed to be new to the listener, *a/an* is used: *a guitar* or *an ostrich*. If the noun refers to something the listener has already heard about or can be expected to know, *the* is used: *the guitar* or *the ostrich*. Hence a noun will often have *a* the first time it occurs, *the* the second time: *a dog came in and sniffed around; then the dog went out. A* shows that the dog has not been seen before; *the* that it is already identified.

Plural nouns are slightly different; something new requires Ø, *Ø guitars* (or indeed *some guitars*) or *Ø ostriches*, something already known has *the*, *the guitars* and *the ostriches*. Choosing the right article to convey whether something is known or unknown to the listener means knowing whether the noun is countable or uncountable and whether it is singular or plural. This aspect of meaning is sometimes called Hearer Knowledge in SLA research.[21]

Another dimension of meaning of articles is whether the noun refers to a specific thing or to something in general. An example might be *A pretty girl is like a melody* (Irving Berlin song). It's not a specific girl or a specific melody that is being talked about but any pretty girl and any melody – a generic girl and a generic melody. This is a different meaning from *A/the pretty girl came in the room* where a specific person is meant. This is often called 'specific' or 'non-generic' reference in SLA research.

The complexity of the article system is that these two dimensions of meaning are conveyed by three articles (and *some*) which behave differently with singular and plural nouns. Derek Bickerton has claimed that the human mind contains two principles: specific versus non-specific reference, and presupposed versus non-presupposed.[22] English articles are one expression of this built-in attribute of the human mind. The box gives a rough summary of the article system (including *some* for one of the gaps), which is handled by researchers in a multitude of ways; a full version of a grammatical system for determiners can be found in Halliday's *An Introduction to Functional Grammar.*[2]

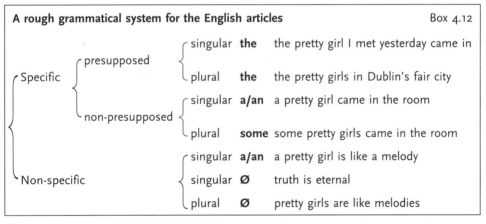

A rough grammatical system for the English articles   Box 4.12

Specific	presupposed	singular	**the**	the pretty girl I met yesterday came in
		plural	**the**	the pretty girls in Dublin's fair city
	non-presupposed	singular	**a/an**	a pretty girl came in the room
		plural	**some**	some pretty girls came in the room
Non-specific		singular	**a/an**	a pretty girl is like a melody
		singular	**Ø**	truth is eternal
		plural	**Ø**	pretty girls are like melodies

Learning an article system in a second language involves knowing when to use the articles to express the appropriate meanings, which is particularly difficult when the first language lacks articles altogether. Box 4.13 collects some sentences written by Chinese students of English. Chinese does not have articles but expresses the meanings in other ways.

Chinese students' articles   Box 4.13

I used to be cook in peking hotel.

Chinese women becam very important role in production field.

I had taken the education . . .

. . . in Taiwan the food is more cheaper.

Once I went to supermarket.

I only got most of my knowledge from the books and films.

American is high technology orientation country.

After the introducing of computer, . . .

. . . computer take the new life into our world.

Two typical problems are seen in the box. One is leaving out articles, as in *to supermarket* and *in peking hotel*. With other parts of grammar, leaving something out may not be crucial. Unfortunately, however, omitting an article looks just the same as the zero Ø article that is part of the English article system. It suggests, say, that supermarkets and hotels are general categories rather than specific places. Indeed a handful of nouns have a precise meaning difference involved in the *the/Ø* contrast. *I am going to school* means I am getting educated; *I am going to the school* means travelling to a particular school, not necessarily for education – a child goes to school, the postie delivers letters to the school. In general, omission of English articles by L2 users is common when the first language does not have articles, a case of L1 transfer.

The reverse problem is using *a* or *the* where Ø is expected: *knowledge from the books and films* and *take the new life into our world.* This may convey the wrong meaning by suggesting that specific books are meant rather than books in general or some particular form of life rather than general inspiration. In terms of the meaning reflected in article choice, Russian and Korean learners overuse both *the* with specific meaning and *a* with non-specific meaning.[23] It is not just presence or absence of articles that is important but how the whole article system is used.

While English has articles, other languages like Japanese have classifiers. These are used for counting objects to show what kind of object is involved. In some ways classifiers resemble the English phrases for counting uncountables, *a glass of water, a pile of sand,* etc. In English, mass nouns such as *water* and *clay* cannot be directly modified by numerals – *a water* and *20 clays* are virtually impossible – but have to be quantified through particular classifiers – *a glass of water* and *a ball of clay.* Count nouns such as *book* and *day* have no such restriction – *a book, 20 days.* Japanese does not normally express quantity: *koko ni hon ga aru* ('here is book'), *koko ni mizu ga aru* ('here is water'). When quantity is expressed, the noun is preceded by the numeral and a classifier *koko ni issatsu no hon ga aru* (literally 'here is one-classifier book') versus *koko ni ippai no mizu ga aru* ('here is one-classifier water').

Clearly this means problems for English learners of Japanese, who have to learn a fair number of classifiers along with the noun classes they go with, and problems for Japanese learners of English, who have to learn a system with a limited number of articles and noun classes but some subtle and complex meaning distinctions.

It also shows how grammar goes along with particular ways of thinking. As Japanese speakers don't have a mass and count distinction while English speakers do, the Japanese see things in terms of uncountable substances, the English see them as shapes. Show people the cork pyramid in Box 4.14 and ask them to say which of the two other objects goes with it; English people say the plastic pyramid, Japanese the piece of cork.

Shapes versus substances   Box 4.14

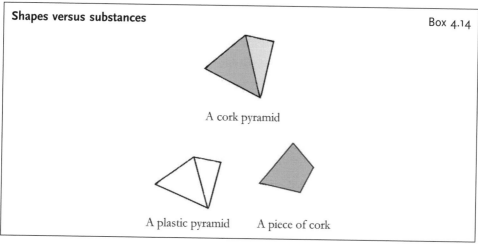

A cork pyramid

A plastic pyramid   A piece of cork

Those who believe language affects thinking claim the differences between English articles and Japanese nouns makes English speakers think differently from Japanese speakers.[24] Learning another language may make you think differently, as seen in Topic 1. Indeed Japanese who have been in England longer than three years tend to switch towards the English preference for shapes in this task. Acquiring another grammar may affect not only your first language but also your overall way of thinking.

This chapter has shown that grammar plays an important role in second language acquisition, perhaps less obvious than vocabulary or phonology, but, without a skeleton of grammar to hold the words and sounds together, the sentence would fall apart. Throughout we have seen that grammar is not pure form but expresses particular meanings of its own – the major relationships of who is doing what to whom and the concepts of number, gender and specific reference. Very little if any of the mental grammar we know and use for processing language is unnecessary and conveys no meaning. Grammar is as tied to meaning as vocabulary – but it is meaning of a different and more subtle type: grammatical meaning. Hence debates about form versus meaning in SLA research are beside the point. Grammar is there to convey a certain kind of meaning; an element of grammar that has no meaning for its users would soon vanish from a language, as for example the English pronoun system seems to be disappearing in expressions such as *between you and I* and *John and me went out*; a *Guardian* columnist indeed used the phrase *like I.*

Summary   Box 4.15

- *Stages.* L2 learners acquire grammatical morphemes in a similar sequence, as is true for other grammatical areas.
- *Word order processing.* L1 preferences affect L2 processing and vice versa.
- *The article system* involves complex meaning issues which may cause the L2 learner to 'think' differently, whichever language is involved.

Postscript   Box 4.16

What do you think of grammar in second language acquisition now? Mark your opinion on these scales.

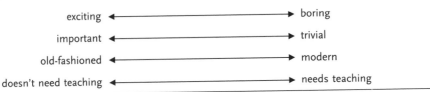

exciting ←——————————→	boring
important ←——————————→	trivial
old-fashioned ←——————————→	modern
doesn't need teaching ←——————————→	needs teaching

Answers to L2 student essays (see Box 4.5, p. 60)   Box 4.17

First languages
(1)   . . . we have many book about him **Farsi**
(2)   . . . one of the most important things in the American social relationship is a punctuality
      Bahasa Indonesia
(3)   I have experienced myself many culture shocks **French**
(4)   They proud of it very much **Japanese**
(5)   Other problem not commun now is the tenant, who wants finish with the problem shoot him
      or going to the war and is xxxxx his own gun **Spanish**
(6)   I just eight months before here **Urdu**
(7)   . . . Because then have you to speak in every situation (in this language,) **German**
(8)   The government try to bring the most advantage things to develope the nation **Arabic**

Further reading

Most standard introductions to second language acquisition will cover the area of grammar, such as:

Cook, V.J. (2008) *Second Language Learning and Language Teaching*, 4th edition. London: Arnold.

Mitchell, R., Myles, F. and Marsden, E. (2013) *Second Language Learning Theories*, 3rd edition. London: Routledge.

Ortega, L. (2009) *Understanding Second Language Acquisition*. London: Hodder Education.

References

1. Biber, D., Johansson, S., Leech, G., Conrad, S. and Finegan, E. (1999) *Longman Grammar of Spoken and Written English*. Harlow: Longman.

2. Halliday, M.A.K. and Matheissen, C. (2004) *An Introduction to Functional Grammar*, 3rd edition. London: Hodder Educational.

3. Cook, V.J. (1993) *Linguistics and Second Language Acquisition*. New York: St Martin's Press.

4. Bruner, J. (1983) *Child's Talk*. Oxford: Oxford University Press.

5. Selinker, L. (1972) Interlanguage. *International Review of Applied Linguistics* X (3), 209–231.

6. Klein, W. and Perdue, C. (1997) The basic variety (or: Couldn't natural languages be much simpler?). *Second Language Research* 13 (4), 301–347.

7. Hirata-Edds, T. (2011) Influence of second language Cherokee immersion on children's development of past tense in their first language, English. *Language Learning* 61 (3), 700–733.

8. Jarvis, S. (2003) Probing the limits of L2 effects in the L1: A case study. In V.J. Cook (ed.) (2003) *L2 Effects on the L1*, 81–102. Clevedon: Multilingual Matters.

9. Jarvis, S. and Pavlenko, A. (2009) *Crosslinguistic Influence in Language and Cognition*. Abingdon: Routledge.

10. Schmid, M. (2006) *Language Attrition*. Cambridge: Cambridge University Press.

11. Brown, R. (1973) *A First Language: The Early Stages*. London: Allen and Unwin.

12. Dulay, H.C. and Burt, M.K. (1974) Natural sequences in child second language strategies. *Language Learning* 24, 37–53.

13. Hannan, M. (2004) A Study of the Development of the English Verbal Morphemes in the Grammar of 4–9 year Old Bengali-Speaking Children in the London Borough of Tower Hamlets. PhD thesis. University of Essex.

14. Krashen, S. (1981) *Second Language Acquisition and Second Language Learning*. Oxford: Pergamon.

15. Pienemann, M. (1998) *Language Processing and Second-Language Development: Processability Theory*. Amsterdam: John Benjamins.

16. Wode, H. (1981) *Learning a Second Language*. Tübingen: Narr.

17. Bates, E. and MacWhinney, B. (1982) Functionalist approaches to grammar. In E. Wanner and L. Gleitman (eds) (1982) *Language Acquisition: The State of the Art*. Cambridge: Cambridge University Press.

18. Kilborn, K. and Cooreman, A. (1987) Sentence interpretation strategies in adult Dutch-English bilinguals. *Applied Psycholinguistics* 8, 415–431.

19. Issidorides, D.C. and Hulstijn, J. (1992) Comprehension of grammatically modified and non-modified sentences by second language learners. *Applied Psycholinguistics* 13 (2), 147–161.

20. Cook, V.J., Iarossi, E., Stellakis, N. and Tokumaru, Y. (2003) Effects of the second language on the syntactic processing of the first language. In V.J. Cook (ed.) *Effects of the Second Language on the First*. Clevedon: Multilingual Matters, 214–233.

21. Ekiert, M. (2007) The acquisition of grammatical marking of indefiniteness with the indefinite article *a* in L2. *English Teachers College, Columbia University Working Papers in TESOL & Applied Linguistics* 7 (1), 1–43.

22. Bickerton, D. (1981) *Roots of Language*. Karoma: Ann Arbor.

23. Ionin, T., Ko, H. and Wexler, K. (2004) Article semantics in L2-acquisition: The role of specificity. *Language Acquisition* 12, 3–69.

24. Cook, V.J., Bassetti, B., Kasai, C., Sasaki, M. and Takahashi, J.A. (2006) Do bilinguals have different concepts? The case of shape and material in Japanese L2 users of English. *International Journal of Bilingualism* 2, 137–152.

5

How Do People Learn to Write in a Second Language?

Vivian Cook

For a hundred years or more linguists and language teachers alike have been more concerned with the spoken language than with the written and so have paid little attention to how L2 learners acquire a new writing system or to the long-lasting difficulties many have with the sheer mechanics of L2 writing. Yet written language is a key means of communication for many L2 users now that emails are used for all purposes of language, whether serious or frivolous, and that social communication takes place through Twitter, Facebook, texting and the like. Written language is not just for reading novels and textbooks and writing formal letters, academic assignments or business reports.

Starter   Box 5.1

How often do you:

- read a book?   never ☐   sometimes ☐   once a week ☐   every day ☐
- read a newspaper?   never ☐   sometimes ☐   once a week ☐   every day ☐
- read a street sign   never ☐   sometimes ☐   once a week ☐   every day ☐
- read an email?   never ☐   sometimes ☐   once a week ☐   every day ☐
- read a tweet?   never ☐   sometimes ☐   once a week ☐   every day ☐

Quotations   Box 5.2

The written symbol extends infinitely, as regards time and space, the range within which one mind can communicate with another; it gives the writer's mind a life limited by the duration of ink, paper, and readers, as against that of his flesh, and blood body. *Samuel Butler*

Those who write as they speak, even though they speak well, write badly. *Comte de Buffon*

Punctuation is cold notation; it is not frustrated speech; it is typographic code. *Robert Bringhurst*

Spelling is one of the outward and visible marks of a disciplined mind. *James J. Kilpatrick*

Don't write naughty words on walls if you can't spell. *Tom Lehrer*

Undoubtedly many people consider correct spelling to be a badge of education and politeness. Spell 'receive' as 'recieve' or 'accommodation' as 'accomodation' and you will offend them. Yet objectively a spelling mistake is no worse than a pronunciation mistake or a grammatical mistake. The first duty is to get the reader to comprehend what you are trying to say and mistakes only matter to communication if they convey the wrong meaning.

However, spelling mistakes make far more of an impact than they logically deserve. The most revolutionary of thinkers or poets makes quite certain that what they write appears in print free of spelling mistakes. The daily newspapers in England pounced with glee on Gordon Brown when he sent a handwritten letter of condolence to a dead soldier's mother that she felt was disrespectful because he misspelled 'Mrs Janes' as 'Mrs James', 'greatest' as 'greatst', 'your' as 'you', and 'colleagues' as 'colleagus' – whether this is fair criticism of the then Prime Minister is another matter as he has poor eyesight, illegible handwriting and was after all taking the time to write a letter himself. (Note that in this chapter examples of spelling are given in single quotation marks.) Spelling checkers would easily have corrected these errors. This is not to say that they are a complete solution as they generate errors of their own like 'form' for 'from' and 'Cupertino' for 'cooperation', the famous mistake that led NATO in 2003 to announce 'the Cupertino with our Italian comrades proved to be very fruitful', the simple explanation being that Cupertino is the town in California where Apple is based and so highly important for spelling checkers.

To familiarise yourself with the types of English spelling mistakes that L2 users of English make, try the test in Box 5.3. Answers are in Box 5.18 on p. 87. Various other spelling tests are online at http://homepage.ntlworld.com/vivian.c/TestsFrame.htm.

What's their first language?					Box 5.3

If people's accents show where they come from, this should also be true of their spelling mistakes. See if you can recognise which first languages these people speak from their spelling.

	Spanish	Chinese	Arabic	Japanese	English
(1) essenciall	☐	☐	☐	☐	☐
(2) aquir	☐	☐	☐	☐	☐
(3) tradditional	☐	☐	☐	☐	☐
(4) empasises	☐	☐	☐	☐	☐
(5) pronounciation	☐	☐	☐	☐	☐
(6) Engilish	☐	☐	☐	☐	☐
(7) adress	☐	☐	☐	☐	☐
(8) well-payed	☐	☐	☐	☐	☐
(9) puneshments	☐	☐	☐	☐	☐
(10) tryed	☐	☐	☐	☐	☐
(11) snorring	☐	☐	☐	☐	☐
(12) ram (lamb)	☐	☐	☐	☐	☐
(13) youngesters	☐	☐	☐	☐	☐
(14) syllubus	☐	☐	☐	☐	☐
(15) neccesary	☐	☐	☐	☐	☐

Why then do nearly all of us make spelling mistakes from time to time, whether children, adult native speaker or L2 users? Some of the possibilities are:

Pronunciation

The ways that L2 users pronounce the sounds of the language may differ from those of 'standard' native speakers. L2 users transfer their spoken accent to a spelling accent. An example is seen in the Japanese spelling 'ram' for 'lamb', reflecting the well-known Japanese problem of distinguishing the 'l' and 'r' sounds of English. Further examples are 'ad-rib' for 'ad-lib' and a Tokyo restaurant that offers 'blunch' rather than 'brunch'. So the speaker's spoken accent may come across in their spellings.

This applies as much to native children learning English as to L2 users. Children in Essex spell 'bath' as 'barf' and 'feather' as 'fever' because in their accent /θ/ and /ð/ are pronounced /f/ and /v/; they spell 'wall' as 'waw' and 'pool' as 'pow' because they have a 'vocalic /l/' where /w/ replaces /l/ at the ends of words – a common feature of present day Southern British English found in my own accent, having lived in Essex for some time. Spelling is usually taught through links between the letters and the sounds of the standard accent – in England Received Pronunciation (RP), which is spoken by a small minority of people. So a child with an Essex accent has to learn to spell with an RP accent; they learn to read and write through a second dialect, just as Swiss children who speak Swiss German learn to read and write in High German.[1]

Some spelling mistakes reflect the specific problems of speakers of particular first languages, as seen in the Japanese 'l~r'. Or in the Arabic mistakes 'bicture' (picture) and 'Urob' (Europe) which show the lack of a /p~b/ contrast in Arabic. Others are to do with common problems of learning a second language. A widespread difficulty with English is the 'th' /ð~θ/ sounds reflected in such L2 spellings as Spanish 'faitfully' and Chinese and Italian 'menthal' (mental).

Writing system

Writing systems differ in the direction in which the letters or characters are written on the page. Traditional Chinese and Japanese writing is in vertical columns from right-to-left; Arabic and Urdu are written from right-to-left in rows; French and German are written from left-to-right. The direction of writing affects everything from the hand movements involved in forming the letters to the shapes of the letters themselves, to the order in which the pages of books are turned over (front-to-back or back-to-front). Most crucially, direction affects how our eyes travel along the line when reading, a basic element in our literacy skills. Going from a writing system with one direction to a second writing system with another is in itself a demanding task; Arabic children in England, for example, often try to write Arabic from left-to-right.

Samples of writing systems with different directions Box 5.4

Japanese (columns)   Persian (right-to-left)   French (left-to-right)

Indeed, direction has a broader effect on how we perceive the world. Children who read Arabic place pictures of events in a different order from those who read English.[2] Think of the problems with advertisements for slimming cures etc., where the terribly fat person is on the left, the wonderfully slim person on the right. Presumably in right-to-left systems this would show the terrible effects of the cure rather than its success.

Sound correspondences for English vowel letters   Box 5.5

a bait, wag, talkative, father, anaemia, daughter, many, aisle, boat, aerial, beauty, cauliflower, artistically (silent)
e ten, cedar, be, kidney, offer, bureau, eight, lewd, pace (silent)
i bit, bite, legible, auntie, sign, dirt, business (silent)
o phone, dog, memoir, door, book, word, youth, ludicrous, cow, tough, flour, boy
u but, fruit, burn, use, full, guest (silent)
y yes, martyr, ratify, nylon, funny

Letter/sound correspondences

The core principle of many writing systems is that the letters correspond to sounds. This requires a set of conventions that say that the sound /s/ can correspond to the letters 's' in 'see' or 'c' in 'cell', and that the letter 'f' corresponds to the sound /f/, except in the word 'of' where it corresponds to /v/. When the letters and sounds of a writing system are in one-to-one correspondence with each other, people often call it a 'phonetic' language, though this has little to do with the usual meaning of 'phonetic'. Instead linguists prefer to call such writing systems 'shallow' or 'transparent'. The writing systems of languages like Finnish and Italian are shallow in that each sound of the language virtually always corresponds to the same letter of the alphabet and each letter always corresponds to the same sound, with few exceptions.

Some writing systems, however, do not have iron-cast one-to-one correspondences between sounds and letters but multiple correspondences in both directions; these are called 'deep' or 'opaque' systems. The deepest of all is probably Japanese kanji since there is no connection between a character and the morpheme it represents. You cannot work out that 猫 is read out as 'neko' ('cat') from the character itself: you either know its spoken form or you don't. Just as in English you either know what '&' and '£' correspond to or you don't. Indeed the '=' sign in '2+2=4' can be read aloud as 'is', 'are', 'equal', 'equals', 'makes' or 'make'. So the artist formerly known as Prince created a problem when he decreed his name was now ♀ as no-one could work out how to say it (the solution being to refer to him as the Artist Formerly Known As Prince; Tafkap for short).

It is obvious that an alphabet of 26 letters cannot correspond directly to the 44 phonemes of English without something having to give. So one letter may correspond to many sounds: 't' corresponds to different sounds in 'bathe, bath, catch, blitz, picture, digestion, ingratiate, trip' etc., with only the 't' in 'trip' having the standard correspondence with /t/. And one sound can correspond to many letters; the phoneme /k/ corresponds to the letter 'c' in 'came', 'k' in 'kill', 'ck' in 'back', 'ch' in 'choir', 'cc' in 'according', 'x' in 'axe' and 'qu' in 'quay'. Pairs of letters may correspond to single phonemes, 'wh' to /w/ in 'when' or 'ng' to /ŋ/ in 'sing' or even trios 'tch' for /tʃ/ in 'catch'. Some letters are 'silent' in that they do not have a direct sound correspondence. Silent 'e' in 'dime' shows the preceding vowel is long /ai/ compared to 'dim' with a short /ɪ/; silent 'u' in 'guest' shows a 'hard' /g/ compared with the soft /ʒ/ in 'gesture'. English is a fairly deep writing system in which the correspondence between sound and letters is far from straightforward.

Some sound correspondences for English consonants   Box 5.6

C   <u>c</u>ar, <u>c</u>ell, <u>ch</u>ef, <u>ch</u>oir, <u>ch</u>ief, o<u>c</u>ean, <u>sc</u>issors (silent)
D   ba<u>d</u>, ba<u>dg</u>er, wat<u>ch</u>e<u>d</u>, san<u>d</u>wich (silent)
G   <u>g</u>ot, wa<u>g</u>e, sabota<u>g</u>e, <u>g</u>nat (silent)
L   <u>l</u>eft, co<u>l</u>onel, fo<u>l</u>k (silent)
S   <u>s</u>ee, die<u>s</u>, <u>s</u>ugar, illu<u>s</u>ion, i<u>s</u>land (silent)
T   <u>st</u>op, <u>th</u>em, <u>th</u>eory, ca<u>tch</u>, na<u>t</u>ion, equa<u>t</u>ion, buffe<u>t</u> (silent)
U   b<u>u</u>t, fr<u>ui</u>t, b<u>u</u>rn, <u>u</u>se, f<u>u</u>ll, g<u>u</u>est (silent)
W   <u>w</u>ind, <u>w</u>ho, <u>w</u>rite (silent)
X   se<u>x</u>, <u>X</u>ena, e<u>x</u>ist
Y   <u>y</u>es, mart<u>y</u>r, rati<u>fy</u>, n<u>y</u>lon, funn<u>y</u>

Spelling reformers frequently lament the inconsistency of English spelling, compared with the simplicity of shallow writing systems like Finnish and Italian; but there's nothing much anybody can do about it. Attempts to make a new alphabet in which each letter would link unambiguously to one sound have always failed, for instance the Shavian alphabet that won a prize set up in George Bernard Shaw's will for a new alphabet for English.[3] Indeed new systems lose their transparency over the years; the Finnish and Italian systems were both standardised in the 19th century and have had little time to become opaque; English goes back a thousand years, leading to such oddities as 'yacht' /jɒt/, 'lieutenant' (/leftenənt/ in British English) and 'Cholmondeley' (pronounced /tʃʌmlɪ/ 'chumley').

L2 learner's mistakes are often caused by the correspondence rules of their first language. So the Spanish spellings 'essenciall' and 'neccessary' tell us something about how the letters 'c~s' are used in Spanish. This is particularly important when learners switch between shallow writing systems like Spanish and deep writing systems like English. Going between two alphabetic sound-based systems is not necessarily easy when the depth varies.

In English, there is a particular issue with the letter-sound correspondences for unstressed spoken vowels. In many words, unstressed vowels are pronounced as schwa /ə/ despite being spelled with 'a' in 'relev<u>a</u>nt', 'e' 'independ<u>e</u>nt', 'i' 'defin<u>i</u>te', 'o' 'pers<u>o</u>n' or 'u' 'ultimat<u>u</u>m'. The reader has to remember how the unstressed vowel is written in each word, calling up a visual memory of the individual word rather than applying a correspondence rule linking letters and sounds. Similar problems arise in French. For example the sequence /parlɛ/ can be spelled 'parlait, parlais, parlaient' while /parle/ can be spelled as 'parlé, parlée, parlés, parlées, parler, parlez'.[4]

Sound-based writing systems also differ over the kinds of sounds that they represent in symbols. English and French use correspondence rules for linking letters to phonemes; the English phoneme /l/ corresponds to the letter 'l' in 'lens'; the French /ʒ/ phoneme corresponds to the letter 'g' in 'gens' and so on. The Arabic writing system, however, only represents consonant phonemes, reserving vowels for some specialised writing genres like children's books. Arabic learners aren't going to treat the English vowels as seriously as those who come from a first writing system that represents both consonants and vowels, hence mistakes like 'evry', 'havn't' or 'joks'.

Japanese kana characters on the other hand correspond to whole syllables rather than single phonemes: か corresponds to the syllable 'ka', さ to 'sa', き to 'ki' and し to 'si'. Though Arabic letters, English letters and Japanese kana are all linked to sounds, they embody different concepts about whether the crucial sounds are consonants alone, consonants and vowels, or syllables. These writing systems actually fit the phonologies of the two languages rather well; Japanese has a limited number of syllables so that only 48 kana symbols are needed (though there are two sets of kana used for different kinds of words), while English has a large number of syllables and would not work well in a syllabic script. The first writing system we learn infiltrates our language in various ways; indeed some linguists claim that only people brought up with an alphabetic first writing system would have come up with the very concept of the phoneme; phonological theory might have been based on the syllable if it had originated in Japan.

Syllable structure

As we have just seen, the syllable plays an important role in most writing systems. Languages have different ways of putting sounds and letters into syllables, particularly how consonants may be combined. Japanese syllables have to have a single consonant (C) and vowel (V), a CV structure, as we see in 'ka ki sa' above and as one can readily detect in any Japanese word – 'Miyazaki', 'Yokohama', 'Mitsubishi', etc. Other languages have a consonant-vowel-consonant (CVC) structure. Mandarin Chinese can only have one final consonant and it has to be /ŋ/ or /n/, as we readily see in Chinese names 'Chen, Wong, Tsang': Cantonese has four more final consonants such as /m/ 'dimsum' and /k/ 'pakchoi'. English has a CVC structure in which several consonants can occur both initially and finally, 'pin/nip', and many consonant clusters which combine two or more consonants like /str/ 'stress' or /ndz/ 'hands'.

Naturally people who are learning a second language expect it to have a similar syllable structure to their own. Speakers of CV languages learning CVC languages frequently encounter syllables and consonant combinations that are impossible in their first language. A common solution is to pad the syllables out with extra 'epenthetic' vowels, carried over to the written language to make them fit. It can be seen in the Arabic mistakes 'youngesters' and 'puneshments' and the Japanese 'Engilish', where the epenthetic 'e's and 'i's interrupt the consonant sequences 'ngst', 'nshm' and 'ngl', respectively. Indeed the Japanese language has made many English words its own by adding final vowels to the syllables to conform to the Japanese CV syllable structure, as in 'kyatto fuudo' ('catfood'). Some examples are given in Box 5.7 – it should by the way not be assumed that they still have the same meaning as the English word; the Japanese word 'bosu' may come from the English word 'boss' but it means 'gang leader'.

Japanese words taken from English with added vowels Box 5.7

sutoraki : strike	bosu : boss
nekutai : neckties	gurin-piisu : green peas
hotto rain : hotline	taipuraita : typewriter
haado-uea : hardware	puroguraame : programme
doraggu : drugs	happi-endo : happy ending
suteshon : station	seroteepu : sellotape
purintaa : printer	arubamu : photo album
kurippu : paper clip	basuketto : basket

Scripts

Scripts are the ways in which the very shapes of the symbols vary between writing systems. Even the familiar Roman alphabet has some variations, say the Spanish 'ñ', French 'é' or German 'ä'. But a sound-based script can have quite different forms for the letters, like Greek 'Σ' (sigma /s/) or Arabic 'ب' (ba /b/) or Cyrillic 'Ж' (zhe /ʒ/). Switching between writing systems that use the same Roman alphabet does not present learners with grave problems.

We are hardly aware of the labour we had to expend as children on learning how to write the letters of our alphabet. English children are taught to make the letter 'o' in an anti-clockwise fashion with pens, Chinese in a clockwise fashion with brushes. English people write letters like 'E' starting with the vertical stroke and then adding the three horizontal strokes; Chinese start characters with the horizontal strokes and add the vertical last, as seen in the Chinese student's *it*, where the crossbar has clearly been made before the downstroke.[5] The very shapes of our letters give away our first writing system. I used to write a capital 'I' as '𝒥', to the annoyance of my teachers, so I changed it to 'I'. Years later I discovered it was simply a Continental '𝒥' I had picked up in Switzerland as a child. I have, however, stuck to my Continental crossed '7'. We have unconscious engrained handwriting habits that seem virtually untouched by a second language – Greek handwriting is usually recognisable in English for its 'α' in place of 'a'. The problem of recognising and writing the appropriate signs of the second writing system is largely unappreciated.

Reading and writing processes

Some writing systems do not link letters to sounds but characters to meanings; a Chinese dictionary has something like 50,000 characters corresponding to morphemes rather than to words; some 3000 are needed for everyday use. The Chinese character 狗 means 'dog', 川 means 'river', and 大 means 'big'. People who speak different 'dialects' of Chinese have different spoken words for 狗 'dog': in Mandarin it is 'gou3' (the number showing the falling-rising tone), in Hakka 'gieu', and in Min 'gau4'. But all of them know that 狗 means 'dog', however different their spoken words may be – the factor which keeps Chinese a single written language regardless of spoken dialect. Chinese and Japanese are the main languages that use character-based systems, though, as we have seen, Japanese supplements kanji characters with two syllable-based systems called kana and a letter-based system called romaji. Box 5.8 gives an overview of the main writing systems in the world.

Major writing systems of the world	Box 5.8
Sound-based writing	**Meaning-based writing**
Symbols link to speech sounds	Symbols link to meanings
Syllabic: Japanese (kana), many Indian languages (Bengali, Tamil, Gujarati, etc.) (15%)	*Character-based:* Chinese, Japanese (kanji) (34%)
Consonantal: Arabic, Persian, Urdu, etc. (2%)	
Alphabetic: Spanish, Russian, Hindi, etc. (49%)	
(percentages are rough estimates)	

Character-based writing systems thus work on a visual principle rather than a sound-based principle, so that the mind processes them in different ways. This leads to problems for L2 learners who switch from a writing system based on meaning to one based on sounds, and vice versa. In a sense, rather than using their first writing system as a springboard, they have to learn to read all over again, at every level from the way they make the signs or read them to how they store the information about written words in the mind.

There are many kinds of L2 mistakes with English that can be attributed to the meaning/sound divide. One is a tendency to leave out letters, as in the Chinese 'moring' or Japanese 'empasises'. An overall problem is that reading is much slower when using a less familiar mode. Chinese university students in the USA read English at about one-third the speed of their Spanish-speaking peers.[6]

Spelling rules

As well as the correspondence rules for relating sounds and letters, deep writing systems have other rules for well-formed spellings. An example is the three-letter rule in Box 5.9, which affects the spelling and pronunciation of structure words like 'the' and 'for'. Different rules apply to structure words and content words. A structure word may have only one or two letters: 'a', 'I', 'in'; if it starts with 'th', it must correspond to /ð/ 'this'. A content word usually has three or more letters: 'eye', 'inn', 'two' and in content words an initial 'th' must be pronounced /θ/ 'thistle'. Spelling involves knowing grammar as well as sounds: you won't get far with English spelling unless you know, consciously or unconsciously, the difference between content and structure words. But it also shows that you cannot link English letters to sounds in sequence from left-to-right; you don't know how to pronounce 'th' until you see the letters that come after it, say '-is' to get 'this' with a /ð/ or '-istle' to get 'thistle' with a /θ/.

The English three-letter rule   Box 5.9

If a word has only one or two letters like 'a' or 'my', it must be a structure (function) word; a content word can have three letters or more, like 'aim' or 'tintinnabulation'. When a content word and a structure word have the same phonemes, the content word often gets an extra letter:

oh/owe, no/know, or/ore/oar/awe, an/Ann, by/bye/buy, so/sew/sow, be/bee, eye/aye, to/two/too, we/wee, in/inn

A content word that would normally have two letters by correspondence rules sometimes gets a third added to make up the number:

add, axe, egg, ell, odd, ebb, err, ill, owe

Some exceptional content words do have two letters or less as:

go, ax (American style), ox, hi; old spelling of musical notes (do, re, mi, etc.); pi, id, ta; letter names (a, b, c . . . .), acronyms (AA, UN); printer's terms en (–), em (—).

The English spelling rules that undoubtedly give everybody the most trouble concern the doubling of consonant letters. People wrongly add an extra letter as in the native speaker mistake 'tradditional'; they leave out one of the doubled letters as in the Arabic 'adress'; they sometimes do both in the same word as in the Spanish 'neccesary'. The rules for doubling form part of a highly complex system in English for showing the pronunciation of the vowel *preceding* the consonant. Doubling the consonant shows the preceding vowel is short, like /ɒ/ 'comma' /kɒmə/, rather than the longer vowels and diphthongs, such as /əʊ/ 'coma' /kəʊmə/. Hence the single 'l' in 'bile' shows the 'i' is pronounced/aɪ/, the double 'll' in 'Bill' shows the 'i' is pronounced /ɪ/.

Some L2 users' doubling mistakes   Box 5.10

quarreling (German/Arabic), comunicate (German/ Japanese), proffessional (Spanish), oppinnion (Italian), allmost (Chinese), controll (Japanese), misstakes (Japanese), shopps (Chinese), inacessible (French), litle (Chinese)

This interacts with a rule, known as the 'fairy letter' rule to English children: 'The fairy letter "e" waves her wand and makes the preceding vowel say its name'. That is to say, the vowel preceding the consonant must be /ei/ (A), /i:/ (E), /ai/ (I), /əʊ/ (O) or /ju:/ (U), the letternames of the five vowels. This creates pairs such as 'man/mane', 'red/rede', 'pin/ pine', 'con/cone', and 'cut/cute'. The apparently silent 'e' identifies the vowel that precedes it; a 'deep' writing system cannot be read aloud from left-to-right one letter at a time; the reader often has to backtrack to get the right sound correspondence. Indeed sometimes the sound corresponding to a letter has to be delayed till later in the sequence; an example is the '£' in '£200' which has to be said aloud after the 'oo' that actually follow it.

So-called silent letters in deep systems like English are only useless if you insist that every letter needs to correspond to a sound directly. The silent letters may influence the sounds assigned to letters around them rather than having a sound of their own. An English silent 'e' as well as showing the preceding vowel correspondence may inter alia show that final 's' is not plural, 'house', 'goose', and that a word is a surname rather than an ordinary noun: 'moor/Moore', 'wild/Wilde'.

It is often hard to tell an L2 user with one background from another purely from their spelling. Sometimes there may be a clear influence from their first language pronunciation whether phonemes as in 'grobal' (l~r) or syllable structure as in 'Engilish' (extra vowel), sometimes from the first writing system as in Arabic 'joks' (missing vowel). But many mistakes are common to all L2 users: the acquisition of English spelling involves much the same problems for all L2 learners.

The most difficult words for overseas students at English universities to spell in English

Box 5.11

accommodating, because, beginning, business, career, choice, definite, develop, different, describe, government, interest(ing), integrate, kindergarten, knowledge, life, necessary, particular, professional, professor, really, study/student, their/there, which, would

Those commonly misspelt on the web

accommodation, address, beginning, cemetery, definitely, desiccate, ecstasy, independent, irresistible, liaison, millennium, necessary, occurrence, paid, parallel, pronunciation, questionnaire, receive, recommend, referring, separate

---

And indeed for native speakers. Box 5.11 gives some common mistakes. A mistake like 'well-payed' highlights an inconsistency in the way English uses the letters 'y' and 'i' in representing the perfectly regular spoken form 'paid' /peɪd/. A mistake such as 'tradditional' shows the consonant doubling rules are difficult for everyone who uses the English spelling system. A mistake like 'syllubus' shows the difficulties in assigning vowel letters for spoken schwa /ə/. 'Adress' was found from speakers of German, French, Arabic, Italian and Spanish. In other words the English spelling system presents much the same problems for everyone, whether they have learnt it as a first or second writing system.

I once compared the mistakes of English children, English adults and L2 learners using a system devised by the National Foundation for Educational Research.[7] The categories are:

- *insertion:* putting in an extra letter, English 'vocabularly';
- *omission:* leaving out a letter, Greek 'softwar';
- *substitution:* putting one letter in place of another, Malaysian 'catagories';
- *transposition:* reversing the order of two letters, Swiss 'foerigners';
- *grapheme substitution:* using the wrong spelling correspondence, 'thort' (thought);
- other things which don't fit any of the other categories.

The results are seen in Figure 5.1 below.[8]

Omission is about the commonest kind of mistake for all three groups, followed by substitution and insertion. The L2 learners have a disproportionate amount of omissions, the L1 children more grapheme substitutions. Yet in terms of this simple measure, there is little to tell the groups apart. Even in terms of sheer number of mistakes, there is little

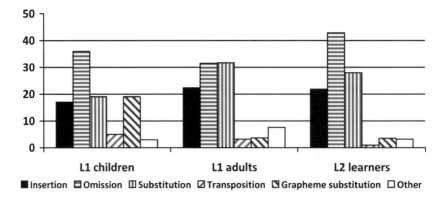

Figure 5.1 Comparison of spelling mistakes by L1 children, L2 users and L1 users (in percent)

between them; the L1 children at the age of 15 make an average of 1.6 mistakes per 10 lines of writing, the L2 adults 1.02. For once L2 learners can boast they are better at spelling than native speakers, even if they are 15-year-old native children.

Questions of punctuation   Box 5.12

(1)   When you read aloud, what do you do about commas and semi-colons?
(2)   How do you know when to put a full stop in your writing?
(3)   What's the point of punctuation?

Punctuation

People often ignore punctuation as if it were obvious and universal. Yet the very punctuation marks themselves vary from one writing system to another. Spanish, for example, has the 'upside-down' punctuation marks '¿' and '¡', cleverly designed by the Real Academia in 1754 to show that a sentence was a question or an exclamation right from its beginning. The modern innovation of the combined question and exclamation marks, the interrobang '‽', has not, however, taken off though it can be found in the computer font Wingdings 2.

Quotation marks also vary in form from one writing system to another: ” ” in Germany but goosefeet « » in Italy; Swiss goosefeet are in reverse » «; Korean Hangul uses ⌈ ⌋. British English and American English styles adopt more or less the opposite policies on when to use double “ ” and single marks ‘ ’. A Chinese full stop is hollow ₒ, a Catalan one is raised · . Learning another writing system often involves learning the actual form of its punctuation marks.

Before proceeding further, try the restoration task in Box 5.13. All punctuation has been removed, including the capital letters.

Restoring punctuation Box 5.13

Restore the punctuation marks to this piece of classic late 19th century prose:

catherine sat alone by the parlour fire sat there for more than an hour lost in her meditations her aunt seemed to her aggressive and foolish and to see it so clearly to judge mrs penniman so positively made her feel old and grave she did not resent the imputation of weakness it made no impression on her for she had not the sense of weakness and she was not hurt at not being appreciated she had an immense respect for her father and she felt that to displease him would be a misdemeanour analogous to an act of profanity in a great temple but her purpose had slowly ripened and she believed that her prayers had purified it of its violence the evening advanced and the lamp burned dim without her noticing it her eyes were fixed upon her terrible plan

Henry James *Washington Square*

The punctuation mark that we most take for granted is effectively invisible but we soon notice when it is missing. In Europe the systematic use of a space to separate words was introduced in the 8th century AD and, according to some, enabled people to read silently for the first time, thus leading to the individualism of the Renaissance as potentially dangerous messages no longer had to be read aloud. Yet, despite their obvious usefulness, word spaces are not found in some alphabetic languages such as Burmese, Thai and Inuktituit. Nor do they occur in character-based scripts such as Chinese, which have a standard space between characters regardless of word divisions. Indeed some linguists regard the very concept of word as an artefact generated by linguists with word-spaced first writing systems. The only practical definition of word for English is 'One or more letters preceded and followed by spaces'. The restoration task above did not cut out word spaces because that would have made it too difficult for a modern reader!

Grammatical punctuation Box 5.14

.   full stop (period) shows the end of a (textual) sentence
; : semi-colon and colon divide the sentence into clauses
,   comma shows the end (and sometimes beginning) of a phrase
_   word-space divides the text into words
-   hyphen connects words into compounds: tea-bag
'   shows inflectional morphemes; *John's*, and abbreviations *isn't*

Phonological punctuation Box 5.15

.   full stop is a long pause
;   semi-colon is a medium pause
,   comma is a short pause
?   question-mark means rising intonation
!   exclamation mark means exclamatory intonation

The perpetual argument about punctuation concerns what it actually stands for. Some say that it is a guide to reading aloud, i.e. phonological. Since the 18th century, English children have been taught some version of Robert Lowth's 1762 rule 'The period is a pause in quantity or duration double of the colon; the colon is double of the semicolon; and the semicolon is double of the comma'.[9] So reading aloud:

>   John laughed. Peter ran.
> there would be a long pause after 'laughed' and 'ran'; reading aloud:
>   John laughed; Peter ran.
> there would be a medium pause after 'laughed'; reading aloud:
>   John laughed, Peter ran.
> there would be a short pause after 'laughed'.

These punctuation marks may well be relevant cues to reading aloud. But, except for newsreaders, parents and children learning to read, reading aloud is not a frequent or indeed important activity. For most reading is in fact silent. Over-emphasis on reading aloud may slow children down from their potential reading speed, which far exceeds their speaking speed.

The alternative view of punctuation is that it helps the reader by marking out the sentences, clauses and phrases of the sentence: its purpose is grammatical. A written sentence can be defined as any stretch of text that starts with a capital letter and finishes with a full stop, question mark or exclamation mark – something that children need years to learn. This makes it differ from the definition of a spoken sentence, which relies on its internal structure, i.e. usually having a main verb and being 'complete'. To illustrate from the first five pages of a single modern novel, *White Teeth* by Zadie Smith, all the following are written sentences:

> Early in the morning, late in the century, Cricklewood Broadway.
> Caps.   Thirty years.   Like that.   Ready?

However familiar the punctuation marks may seem, the L2 learner has the non-trivial task of working out how they are used in the second writing system, certainly if they need to present formal written work to anybody.

Box 5.16 below sums up some of the main factors involved in learning the writing system of a new language.

Summary: Learning a second writing system   Box 5.16

- If the first writing system is sound-based, the second meaning-based, you need to learn to write on quite different principles, processing sounds or meanings visually or phonologically.
- If the writing direction is different between the two writing systems, you have to acquire a different direction, ranging from physical eye-movement to mental ideas of sequence.
- If the first system is based on phonemes, the second on syllables, then you need to acquire a different relationship between sounds and letters.
- If one is based on consonants, the other uses both consonants and vowels, then you need to learn how the correspondences work.
- If both systems are deep, you need to know the complex orthographic rules of the new system.
- If the first writing system is shallow and the second is deep, you need to acquire the idea that spelling is not just one letter/one sound as well as the specific spelling rules.
- If both systems are shallow, you need to acquire the specific sound-letter correspondences for the new system.

Postscript   Box 5.17

What do you think are the sources of any spelling problems you have in your *first* language?

What do you think are the sources of any spelling problems you have in your *second* language?

What if anything do you think can be done about the difficulties that advanced students still have with English spelling?

Answers to 'What's their first language?' (Box 5.3, p. 75)   Box 5.18

Spanish; neccesary, essenciall, pronounciation

Chinese: aquir, tryed, snorring

Arabic: adress, puneshments, youngesters

Japanese: Engilish, empasises, ram (lamb)

English native speaker: tradditional, well-payed, syllubus

The punctuation restored   Box 5.19

Catherine sat alone by the parlour fire – sat there for more than an hour, lost in her meditations. Her aunt seemed to her aggressive and foolish, and to see it so clearly – to judge Mrs. Penniman so positively – made her feel old and grave. She did not resent the imputation of weakness; it made no impression on her, for she had not the sense of weakness, and she was not hurt at not being appreciated. She had an immense respect for her father, and she felt that to displease him would be a misdemeanour analogous to an act of profanity in a great temple; but her purpose had slowly ripened, and she believed that her prayers had purified it of its violence. The evening advanced, and the lamp burned dim without her noticing it; her eyes were fixed upon her terrible plan.

Henry James *Washington Square*

Further reading

General books on writing:

Coulmas, F. (2013) *Writing and Society: An Introduction*. Cambridge: Cambridge University Press.

Clayton, E. (2013) *The Golden Thread: The Story of Writing*. London: Atlantic Books.

Books on English:

Carney, E. (1994) *A Survey of English Spelling*. London: Routledge.

Cook, V.J. (2004) *The English Writing System*. London: Edward Arnold.

Venezky, R.L. (1999) *The American Way of Spelling*. New York: Guilford Press.

Book on L2 writing systems:

Cook, V.J. and Bassetti, B. (eds) (2005) *Second Language Writing Systems*. Clevedon: Multilingual Matters. Chinese edition 2007.

References

1. Schmid, S. (1994) *L'italiano degli spagnoli. Interlingue di immigranti nella Svizzera tedesca.* Milano: Franco Angeli.

2. Tversky, B., Kugelmass, S. and Winter, A. (1991) Cross-cultural and developmental trends in graphic productions. *Cognitive Psychology* 23 (4), 515–557.

3. MacCarthy, P.A.D. (1969) The Bernard Shaw Alphabet. In W. Haas (ed.) (1969) *Alphabets for English*. Manchester: Manchester University Press.

4. Brissaud, C. and Chevrot, P. (2011) The late acquisition of a major difficulty of French inflectional orthography: The homophonic /ê/ verbal endings. *Writing Systems Research* 2 (3), 129–144.

5. Sassoon, R. (1995) *The Acquisition of a Second Writing System*, 89–104. Oxford: Intellect.

6. Haynes, M. and Carr, T.H. (1990) Writing system background and second language reading: A component skills analysis of English reading by native-speaking readers of Chinese. In T.H. Carr and B.A. Levy (eds) (1990) *Reading and its Development: Component Skills Approaches.* San Diego: Academic Press, 375–421.

7. Brooks, G., Gorman, T. and Kendall, L. (1993) *Spelling It Out: The Spelling Abilities of 11- and 15-Year-Olds*. Slough: NFER.

8. Cook, V.J. (1997) L2 users and English spelling. *Journal of Multilingual and Multicultural Development* 18 (6), 474–488.

9. Lowth, R. (1775) *Short Introduction to English Grammar.* Delmar, NY: Scholars' Facsimiles & Reprints, 1979.

6

How Do Attitude and Motivation Help in Learning a Second Language?

David Singleton

Starter Box 6.1

Starter Box 6.1

What are the reasons why you have learnt (or not learnt) another language?
Who or what influenced you in this? Parents? Friends? Teachers? Future jobs? Holiday plans?
Previous encounters with language teaching? . . .
Why would you go to live in another country where you don't speak the language?

Liking and wanting

We all know that positive feelings about an experience or an activity incline us to pursue it, whereas negative feelings do not. If I enjoy watching the films of Quentin Tarantino, I will tend to seek them out at the local video shop or cinema. If I find them too violent or simply boring, however, I will avoid them like the plague. We also know that when we strongly want something, our chances of attaining it are much higher than if we do not. Advice to people trying to give up smoking, for instance, usually includes comments such as those in Box 6.2.

Here's how I stopped smoking Box 6.2

. . . The first thing I have to say to any smoker is, bottom line, *you* have to want it. You can't quit for other people because then your heart isn't fully in it. You are more apt to slip if your heart's not there. Learn the facts about smoking and you'll want to quit. I did. . . .'

It is on the basis of such everyday facts that there has been so much interest in recent years on attitudes and motivation in SLA research. The focus of attitude research has been on learners' attitudes towards the language they are trying to learn, towards the language community and the culture associated with the language in question and towards various aspects and elements of the language learning process. Thus, for example, researchers have investigated how learners feel about the national and/or international status of their target language, how they assess its usefulness to them and how they react to the difficulties it presents. They have explored the extent to which learners have positive or negative perceptions in respect of the users of their target language, in respect of social and political aspects of target language users' way of life, and in respect of the products – music, art, fashion, etc. – of the target language culture. Researchers have, in addition, focused on how learners react to how they engage with the target language, including, for instance, how they respond to their teacher, to the teacher's approach, to the learning materials to which they have access and to particular problems they have with the pronunciation or structure of the language.

Closely linked to the question of attitude is that of motivation, defined in general terms as the impetus to create and sustain intentions and goal-seeking acts,[3] as seen in Box 6.3. Motivation goes beyond having good feelings about a task, and needs to be seen as whatever actually spurs a person on to 'do the job'. Second language researchers have taken an interest in the way in which the drive to get on with learning is sparked and maintained by the individual's curiosity and desire to know more, by their sense of the learning task's relevance to their needs, by their perceptions regarding the likelihood of their succeeding in their efforts, and by their levels of satisfaction with the rewards offered by success in their efforts. Attitude and motivation are seen as crucial in any learning context, including second language learning contexts, because they are seen as determining the extent of a learner's active involvement in learning.

Robert Gardner's 1985 definition of L2 motivation[2]   Box 6.3

... the extent to which the individual works or strives to learn the language because of a desire to do so and the satisfaction experienced in this activity

---

Attitudes

Much attitudinal research has dealt with attitudes among immigrants, and has focused on the question of acculturation – the processes whereby members of one cultural group do or do not adopt the perspectives and behaviour patterns of another. Some of the early discussion of this topic emphasised the importance of both *cultural awareness*, an individual's cultural knowledge of both his/her own community and the host community, and *ethnic loyalty*, an individual's preferences of one cultural orientation over other. Other discussion of acculturation has homed in on communication between immigrant and host communities, analysing the different factors involved: the extent to which there is a predisposition to adapt; conditions obtaining in the host environment; the nature of personal communication between hosts and newcomers; the nature of social communication between the host community and the immigrant community; and kinds of adaptation which emerge.

John Berry proposed a model with four modes of acculturation[4]:

* *assimilation* (willingness to abandon one's cultural identity);
* *integration* (aspiration to becoming a member of both cultures);
* *rejection* (separation) (complete withdrawal from the majority community);
* *deculturation* (loss of identity, marginalisation).

He investigated individual attitudes to the nature of relations with the host community, and perceptions of personal cultural identity (whether to be retained or not), which he believes reflect the particular acculturation mode adopted by an individual.

John Schumann, for his part, linked acculturation to the acquisition of the language of the host community.[5,6] He claimed that success in L2 acquisition depends on the extent and quality of contact between the learner and the target language and culture, which in turn depends on the degree of social and psychological distance between the learner and this language and culture. Social distance in this context refers, among other things, to group attitudes and expectations, while psychological distance refers to immigrants' degree of ease or unease with the target language and culture. Schumann studied Alberto, a Costa Rican migrant to the United States (see Box 6.4), whose interest in and contact with English-speaking Americans was minimal, and whose English was claimed by Schumann to have stabilised at a level which was 'a reduced and simplified form of English'.[5] The operative word here is *stabilised*. L2 learners of English from Spanish-speaking backgrounds routinely produce utterances resembling Alberto's on their way to more English-like forms; Schumann's point is that Alberto seemed not to be on his way anywhere, but to be 'stuck' in his simplified state.

Some of Alberto's utterances   Box 6.4

Negatives

No like walk. No understand all. No is mine.

Interrogatives

What is surance? This is apple? You will come here the next Monday?

Declaratives

It's problem for me. Is necessary. Is very bad, no? (Schumann, 1978)[5]

A major component in a person's attitude towards a language and culture is the set of beliefs which that person holds in relation to the language and culture in question. A migrant to Hungary, for example, may begin the process of getting to grips with Hungarian with the belief that it is a difficult language; or a Costa Rican migrant to the United States like Alberto may approach the culture which presents itself with the belief that English-speaking America is hostile to the Spanish-speaking world. Zehra Gabillon points out that beliefs about a foreign language and its culture appear to influence both the actions and experiences of language learners and to have a significant impact on their attitudes towards the language in question and to play a role in their L2 motivations.[7,8,9] Gabillon continues[7]:

> In the same vein, Castellotti and Moore (2002)[10] claim that social groups' shared images (representations) about other languages and learning these languages can influence learners' attitudes towards other languages and finally their interest in learning these languages.

So attitudes which feed into processes relating to becoming more or less proficient in a particular language derive in part from factors relating to acculturation. However, relevant attitudes may derive from a wide range of other factors too, including the learner's reactions with regard to language study in a formal instructional context – to the actual procedures of formal learning. For example, advocates of the use of various kinds of technology-enhanced instruction have pointed to studies which suggest that students enjoy learning under such conditions, and find it less pressuring than traditional teaching, leading to an improved attitude towards the language-learning task.[11] A fair amount of research has shown that a good experience of and/or success in learning a particular language can bring about favourable attitudes.

Attitudes and experience   Box 6.5

There are some learning situations where many learners have not had sufficient experience of the second language community to have attitudes for or against it. ... [M]any learners of French and German in Great Britain provide an example. In cases such as this, it is probable that attitudes relate more directly to learning as it is experienced in the classroom. (Littlewood, 1984)[14]

For instance, two studies of L2 learners in Great Britain by Burstall *et al.*[12] and Green[13] cited by Littlewood[14] found that attitudes towards the target language community were not really a factor initially, but that the learners who were successful developed favourable attitudes as their learning progressed. Success feeds on success. The notion that formal learners' attitudes are consequent on experience and success/failure, is sometimes known as the 'resultative hypothesis'.[15] It is no doubt just part of the story, but apparently an important (and sometimes neglected) part.

A study carried out by Diane de Saint Léger and Neomy Storch[16] seems to show that L2 classroom learners' perception of themselves as learners – in particular their success as learners – has far-reaching consequences for their general disposition towards the learning task. They investigated how the learners assessed their speaking abilities, and what they thought of their contributions to oral class activities (whole class and small

---

Connecting classroom behaviour with success   Box 6.6

Try these sample questions from De Saint Léger and Storch's questionnaire (adapted)[16] about when you were last learning a language in a classroom.

Classroom behaviour

I asked my classmates questions.	Yes	No	Don't know
I offered my opinion in pair work.	Yes	No	Don't know
I made comments in whole class discussion.	Yes	No	Don't know

Attitudes

Which of the following activities do you find particularly difficult to handle?
> Whole group discussion?
> Small group discussion?
> Pair work?

Speaking ability in a second language

(a) How hard is it for you to express yourself fluently, with little hesitation and pauses?
> Very hard Hard   OK   Easy   Very easy

(b) How hard is it for you to talk in a clear and easily understandable manner?
> Very hard Hard   OK   Easy   Very easy

(c) How hard is it for you to take part in a discussion?
> Very hard Hard   OK   Easy   Very easy

---

group discussions) as well as their attitudes towards these activities. The study went on to look into how perceptions and attitudes influenced the learners' willingness to communicate in the second language. The main source of data was self-assessment questionnaires, seen in Box 6.6, which asked the participants to reflect on their immediate learning environment at various points in the teaching/learning programme and to self-assess their speaking skills. The researchers concluded that the participants' perception of the speaking activities and of themselves as learners in the L2 classroom influenced their willingness to communicate via the second language.

> The findings highlight the complex and dynamic nature of the interplay between self-confidence, anxiety and perception of the learning environment.[16]

On the whole, as learners' self-confidence increased, so did their willingness to use the L2 in class.

Motivation

Attitudes, self-perception, self-confidence and anxiety have long been seen as feeding into the *motivational* factor in the L2 learning process. In the study of L2 learning – as in the study of all learning – motivation is seen as key; and an internet search for motivation will confirm that attitude is very closely associated with it. A recent dip into Google yielded 4,400,000 'hits', for example, for the expression 'attitudes and motivation'. Many of the hits were concerned with L2 learning and teaching – but by no means all, as the sites given in Box 6.7 clearly show. It should perhaps be noted that most of the approaches to be described deal with second language learning in school, with Berry's and Schumann's work being the main exceptions. Hence they are part of educational research, rather than research into bilingualism and multilingualism occurring outside the classroom and so are subject to all the many special factors that need to be kept in mind in studying language acquisition in a classroom.

Summary: Attitudes   Box 6.7

- Berry's acculturation model describes four modes: assimilation, integration, rejection (separation), deculturation.[4]
- Schumann's acculturation model sees acculturation as dependent on the user's contacts and relationships with the target culture.[5]
- The learner's own beliefs play a crucial part in their attitudes.

It is easy enough to see the intuitive connection between attitude and motivation, but motivation goes beyond attitude. I may have an extremely benign attitude towards the Italian language and Italian culture, but unless I can turn that attitude into the taking of steps towards learning the language in question, I shall remain well-disposed but silent in relation to it.

Motivation and attitude outside second language acquisition   Box 6.8

School children's awareness, attitudes and motivation towards 'making things' (mono-zukuri): http://idater.lboro.ac.uk/international-comparison-school-children-awareness-attitudes-and-motivation-towards-making-things-mono-zukuri/

Boxing: http://www.boxingscene.com/motivation/6711.php

Employment: http://www.imaeurope.com/wp-content/uploads/2012/05/ Employee_Employer-attitudes.pdf

Women in the workplace: http://woman.thenest.com/work-attitudes-motivation-workplace-11465.html

Spelling: http://www.eric.ed.gov/ERICWebPortal/search/ detailmini.jsp?_nfpb=true&_&ERICExtSearch_SearchValue_0=EJ724710&ERICExtSearch_SearchType_0=no&accno=EJ724710

Golf: http://ria.ua.pt/handle/10773/7098

Health: http://www.paha.org.uk/Resource/knowledge-attitudes-and-motivations-to-health-2010

There is an abundance of different perspectives on motivation in the context of L2 acquisition. Zoltán Dörnyei[17] reviews a numbers of these approaches, including:

- *Schumann's Acculturation Theory,* already mentioned[5];
- *Gardner's Motivation Theory,*[2] which we shall explore below;
- *Dörnyei and Ottó's process-oriented representation of motivation* as a highly dynamic phenomenon, which we deal with a little later in the chapter[18];
- *Dörnyei and Kormos' treatment of task motivation,* which distinguishes between generalised motives, course-specific motives and task-specific motives, of which we also provide a sketch later[19];
- *Self-determination theory* and its distinction between intrinsic motivation and extrinsic motivation, which is the closing theme of this section.[20,21]

Gardner's Motivation Theory, otherwise known as his socio-educational model,[2] is probably the most frequently cited motivational framework in SLA research. It prominently incorporates an attitudinal dimension conceived under the headings of two types of attitudinally based orientation – labelled *integrative* and *instrumental*. In this scheme *integrative orientation* (see Box 6.9) is characterised by positive attitudes towards the target language group and its way of life and this orientation comes into play when the L2 acquirer aspires to become integrated in some sense with the community that uses the target language.

Integrativeness   Box 6.9

The notion of 'integrativeness' – a desire to learn a language in order to "come closer to the other language community" (Gardner, 2001a: 5)[22] – has been a central concept in language learner motivation for several decades now, influential not just in theory and research but in teaching methodology and materials ... In Gardner's (1985)[2] socio-educational model of second language acquisition, learners who had the characteristic of 'integrativeness' were said to have an integrative orientation (or goal) towards learning the language, favourable attitudes towards the language community, and a general openness towards other groups in general ... (Lamb, 2004)[23]

Instrumental orientation, on the other hand, is seen as characterised by the desire to obtain something practical from studying a second language. It is typical of second language acquisition where there is little or no question of the learner being socially integrated into the community using the target language, such as in a foreign language classroom – especially a classroom which is remote from countries where the target language is used on an everyday basis. The learner's purpose in acquiring the second language in such cases is not related to long-term integration, but has more practical, short-term goals – such as meeting a requirement for school or university matriculation or graduation, applying for a job, or gaining access to material in the second language. To illustrate this instrumentally oriented dimension of motivation, one can cite a study in relation to the learning of English in Japanese high schools conducted by Berwick and Ross.[24] In Japan a respectable mark in English is required for university entrance, whatever the subject(s) selected by the candidate for tertiary level study. Berwick and Ross' results indicated that motivation for studying L2 English peaked in the final year of high school, when students were channelling all their energy into studying for university entrance, and that motivation declined subsequently.

Motivational orientation   Box 6.10

Agree or disagree with these statements about learning another language:

(1) If I study another language, I will be able to interact better with those who speak it.

Strongly disagree	Moderately disagree	Slightly disagree	Don't know	Slightly agree	Moderately agree	Strongly agree
☐	☐	☐	☐	☐	☐	☐

(2) I study another language because it's needed in my future career.

Strongly disagree	Moderately disagree	Slightly disagree	Don't know	Slightly agree	Moderately agree	Strongly agree
☐	☐	☐	☐	☐	☐	☐

(3) If I study another language, I will be able to better understand and appreciate the literature of those who speak it.

Strongly disagree	Moderately disagree	Slightly disagree	Don't know	Slightly agree	Moderately agree	Strongly agree
☐	☐	☐	☐	☐	☐	☐

(4) Studying another language will be useful in me getting a good job.

Strongly disagree	Moderately disagree	Slightly disagree	Don't know	Slightly agree	Moderately agree	Strongly agree
☐	☐	☐	☐	☐	☐	☐

These are loosely adapted from questions in the Gardner test battery.[2] Questions 1 and 3 show your integrative motivation, Questions 2 and 4 your instrumental motivation.

Three qualifications need to be made to the above. First, there is no suggestion that the integrative orientation and the instrumental orientation are mutually exclusive; very often, both are present. For instance, Brown[25] cites the case of international students residing in the United States, who are learning English for academic (that is, instrumental) purposes while at the same time wishing to become integrated with the English-speaking American community and culture. Second, the fact that there is a multitude of communities of native speakers of English (American, Australian, British, Irish, South African, etc.), the fact that English has the status of world lingua franca, and the fact that there are, in consequence, three times as many non-native as native users of English[26] have detached the language to a significant extent from any particular community for its L2 users[27] – English is in many ways untypical of foreign language teaching in general. This renders the notion of integrativeness problematic. Third, it is clear that not all reasons given by learners for wanting to master a particular second language fit easily into Gardner's framework. Oxford and Shearin,[28] for instance, mention the following reasons for studying Japanese as reported by the participants in their research: intellectual curiosity, personal challenge, showing off to peers, fascination with the Japanese writing systems and acquiring a secret code. More reasons why people study a language are seen in Topic 8.

In recent versions of the socio-educational approach,[29] three major variables are seen as operative:

- *Integrativeness* – the level of identification with the target language community and the nature of intentionality with respect to getting closer to this community and its language and culture.
- *Attitudes* – towards the target language and culture, in turn permeating attitudes towards the learning of the target language.
- *Motivation* – that is, effort made to learn the majority language, desire to achieve the intended goal, and positive affect, i.e. enjoying the learning.

These three factors, according to Gardner, are the crucial difference between motivated and unmotivated learners. Gardner posits that, of the above three variables, the critical factor for achievement in L2 acquisition is the third – motivation – while the role of the other two is supportive. While this is a change in emphasis from previous thinking, it is not a radical change, since the other two factors are seen still as having an *importantly* supportive function in the whole scenario. Thus, it remains Gardner's view that integratively motivated learners are the most successful learners, including in areas such as the acquisition of native-like pronunciation.[30]

Gardner's approach sometimes gives the impression that a learner's state of motivation is fairly stable and that the L2 learner enters into the process of coming to grips with the target language with the motivational component already in place and more or less fixed. Language teachers are often discouraged by this conception of motivational realities. They feel there is nothing they can do if their learners have little interest in engaging with the target language and community. For learners of the Irish language in Ireland, for instance, the irrelevance of Irish to everyday communicative needs in places like Dublin and Cork – and indeed most of Ireland (see Boxes 6.11 and 6.12) – is obvious even to young children, and would seem to put a damper on all motivation, whether of an integrative or an instrumental orientation. This appears to present teachers with an irredeemable situation, if they perceive motivation as immutably determined by the learners' initial orientation.

> **Languages spoken in Ireland (Census 2011)[31]**   Box 6.11
>
> | | |
> |---|---|
> | English: | 4,159,277 speakers (extrapolated as figure not given) |
> | Polish: | 119,528 |
> | Irish: | 77,185 mostly living on the west coast |
> | French: | 56,540 |
> | Lithuanian: | 31,635 |
> | German: | 27,342 |
>
> Almost one in three 10- to 19-year-olds answered 'no' to the question 'Can you speak Irish?' Yet Irish is compulsory in all state schools.

Recent research has changed this pessimistic perception somewhat by looking into how motivation levels may change according to circumstances.[18,32] Cook, for instance, notes with respect to classroom-based L2 teaching[33]:

> A particular exercise, a particular topic a particular song may interest the students in the class, to the teacher's delight. ... Motivation in this sense is a short-term affair from moment to moment.

It seems that what happens *in* class may be as important as – sometimes more important than – whatever the learners bring with them through the classroom door on the basis of popular beliefs, conversations with parents or indeed hard knowledge of sociolinguistic facts. Thus, by way of illustration, it has clearly been shown that teachers can promote and sustain higher motivation levels by helping learners to identify short-term goals and to reflect on their progress and achievements. Teachers can, for example, provide learners with self-assessment checklists to identify skill strengths and weaknesses, weekly checklists to track their progress on meeting particular learning goals, and self-reflection tools (e.g. learning diaries) to help them build autonomy and take charge of their learning.[35,36] Nitta and Asano's study of 164 first-year students taking a two-semester general L2 English course at a private Japanese university found that although students' initial motivational states could certainly affect the trajectories of motivational changes in the classroom, a number of social and interpersonal factors within the learning situation, such as teaching styles, intergroup relations, and group cohesiveness, had a significant impact on students' changing desire to learn.[37]

> **Communicative syllabi**   Box 6.12
>
> The communicative-type syllabi now being taught in schools imply that learners who have little or no prospect of eventually integrating into or enacting with the speech community are asked to suspend disbelief and rehearse communicative situations, which can only [be] authentic or valid within the Gaeltacht [areas where Irish is in current use] or in the Irish-speaking networks outside the Gaeltacht.
>
> Efforts in our Irish language classrooms intent on simulating the tourist-type situations so central to communicative pedagogy of more widely-used languages have worn thin with many of our learners. (Ó Laoire, 2005)[34]

Motivation is thus viewed ... as process – in effect, the ongoing process of how the learner thinks about and interprets events in relevant L2-learning and L2-related experience and how such cognitions and beliefs then shape subsequent involvement in learning.[38]

Ema Ushioda's comment is eloquently representative of the 'new wave' of thinking, or at least the new emphasis (since Gardner would say that his views never denied such a dimension).[39]

In any case, it emerges clearly from a wide range of classroom-based studies that an L2 learner's motivation may vary from day to day, from task to task and even from interlocutor to interlocutor. In one exploratory study in this domain, Dörnyei and Kormos looked at ways in which tasks can be researched in the light of motivational and other socio-dynamic variables.[19] The linguistic variables were concerned with the quantity of speech produced, which was argued to reflect task-engagement and thus to constitute an important indicator of involvement. In a follow-up study Dörnyei analysed how the partner's motivation influenced the amount of talk produced.[40] He found that such motivation affected the learner's appraisal and action control processes, and he concluded that task motivation is *co-constructed* by the task participants.

Researchers concur with the experience-based folk-wisdom promulgated by many language-teaching practitioners, according to which using varied and challenging instructional activities can help learners stay focused on and engaged with instructional content. Some research and practical experience suggest that there is an interaction between social factors (e.g. group dynamics, learning environment and partners' motivation) and the L2 learner's attitude, effort, classroom behaviour and achievement.[41] There is also a strong view among both researchers and practitioners in favour of the benefits of providing opportunities for the continuation of second language use when learners are not in class.[42] Project-based learning (see Box 6.13), for example, supplies learners with a bridge between practice in class and practice outside of class. In addition, project-based learning supplies opportunities for learners to work with others to accomplish tasks, using the target language in real-life.[43] In addition, current interest focuses on instructional practices aimed at generating strategies through which learners themselves take control of factors that have an impact on their motivation and learning, such as lack of self-confidence or distractions.[45]

Project-based learning   Box 6.13

As any experienced practitioner knows, there is much more to project-based learning than the simple incorporation of projects into the curriculum. The scope of project-based learning is captured, in some ways, by the many labels given to classroom approaches that incorporate projects:

- Experiential and negotiated language learning.
- Investigative research.
- Project approach or project-based approach.
- Project work. (Stoller, 2006)[44]

In this connection it is pertinent to mention a general motivational distinction made by, among others, Deci and Ryan[20] and Vallerand[21] between *intrinsic* motivation and *extrinsic* motivation. Intrinsic motivation is seen as occurring when the learning activity and the learning environment elicit motivation in the learner. The notion is that teachers do not motivate students but rather through their teaching create opportunities that can evoke motivation in students. The following sets of circumstances exemplify conditions which seem to be favourable to the triggering of intrinsic motivation:

- when the purposes of learning and what the learning delivers are meaningful to the learner;
- when the learning is perceived by the learner as in itself of importance;
- when the learning gives the sense of achieving valued accomplishments;
- when the learning helps the learner in the process of integrating themselves with a wider community;
- when the learning helps to promote self-awareness.

Extrinsic motivation is defined in terms of motivation deriving from outside regulation. Most frequently in this context the talk is of 'punishments' and 'rewards' – administered, for example, via a marking system or through parental encouragement and pressure.

Intrinsic motivation and extrinsic motivation are concepts which have wide application with regard to learning in general. In relation to second language learning, intrinsic motivation has been connected by some researchers with the concept of *learner autonomy*, the notion that successful L2 learners are those that take responsibility for their own learning. For Ema Ushioda '[a]utonomous learners are by definition self-motivated learners'.[46] Ushioda sees two types of motivation as interacting with autonomy: intrinsic motivation, when learners want to learn for the kinds of reasons listed above, and self-motivation, when learners develop the capacity and the will to cope with setbacks and challenges. In fact, both of these can be characterised as intrinsic on a broad definition.

> Thus she considers autonomy to be part of motivation because a learner will not learn how to regulate his motivation unless he wants to and until he sees himself as the agent of his learning and of his motivation – i.e., he must be given autonomy. Ushioda ... considers that both theories of autonomy and theories of motivation are directly concerned with the whole process of L2 learning, whatever the learner's proficiency level, length of learning experience, degree of autonomy, and level of motivation. (p. 107)[47]

Extrinsic motivation, on the other hand, is not generally seen as vitally related to the learner's capacity to develop self-determination or independent thinking. One view is, however, that motivation which is not intrinsic may be seen as not monolithically the outcome of some other person's intervention or some imposed system of regulation. Dörnyei (p. 78)[48] cites Noels *et al.*,[49] who talk about amotivated learning, who discuss intrinsically motivated learning and who discuss otherwise motivated learning in terms of 'regulation', which is:

(a) 'external' ('coming entirely from external sources such as rewards or threats');
(b) 'introjected' ('externally imposed rules that the student accepts as norms he/she should follow so as not to feel guilty'); and
(c) a kind of regulation with which the student has 'identified' (engaging in an activity 'because he/she highly values and identifies with the behaviour, and sees its usefulness').

This third kind of 'regulated' motivation blurs into the dimension of intrinsic motivation which relates to accomplishment and the sensations arising from attempting to master a task or achieve a desired goal.

Summary: Some types of motivation   Box 6.14

- *Integrative*: the desire 'to come closer to the other language community'.
- *Instrumental*: the desire to get something practical out of second language learning.
- *Intrinsic*: being motivated by the learning situation itself.
- *Extrinsic*: being motivated by rewards and punishments from others.
- *Amotivation*: lack of motivation.
- *Demotivation*: caused by conflict, resentment and disaffection.

In situations where teachers and/or the ways in which learning is regulated are very obviously in firm control of all aspects of learners' encounters with the target language (or whatever else the object of study may be), the attempt to impose an exclusively or predominantly extrinsic motivation has some chance of yielding positive results. In situations, however, where the learners are utterly convinced of the correctness and viability of their own perspectives, and that their rights are equal to the person or the system regulating the learning regime (distributing the rewards and punishments and so on), the outcome may be entirely different. In the latter case, there is clearly a high probability of conflict, resentment and disaffection – in a word *de*motivation.

Present and future directions

The shortcomings of most approaches to L2 motivation in second language acquisition to date, as Ushioda and Dörnyei point out, is that they have not taken sufficient account of 'the dynamic and situated complexity of the learning process or the multiple goals and agendas shaping learner behaviour'.[50] Acknowledging this deficiency, the move in motivational research is increasingly towards 'a focus on the situated complexity of the L2 motivation process and its organic development in interaction with a multiplicity of internal, social, and contextual factors'. In other words, there is now a preoccupation with perspectives from dynamic systems (the idea that languages are never static systems, always changing) and complexity theory (the idea that such systems organise themselves into more complex forms over time),[51,52] which are very much part of contemporary thinking about second language acquisition and multilingualism. It has long been recognised that L2 motivation research has had a somewhat marginalised position within SLA research, because of its virtual silence on the question of how the psychology of motivation relates – beyond general learning outcomes – concretely and in detail to the processes of second language development. The question now is whether the new direction that motivation research appears to be taking, including its current flirtation with complexity theory, will in any real sense begin to remedy its isolation.

Despite the new directions, Gardner's original socio-educational insights have not gone away. In particular, the importance of integrativeness is still very much with us, and has been reinforced by findings from studies in which an integrative factor appeared to emerge strongly.[40,53] Zoltán Dörnyei, who is sceptical about the separability of the integrative and instrumental orientations (cf. earlier discussion), has attempted, drawing on the psychological theory of possible selves, to re-conceptualise integrativeness within a framework which takes the self, and in particular how the learner thinks about his/her future self, as a key explanatory element in the endeavour to make sense of the multiplicity of claims that co-exist in this area.

> The central concept in the L2 Motivational Self System is the *ideal self*. ... A complementary concept is the *ought-to self*. ... A basic assumption ... is that if proficiency in the target language is part and parcel of one's ideal or ought-to self, this will act as a powerful motivator to learn the language because of our psychological desire to reduce the discrepancy between our current self and possible future selves.[54]

This view of the 'L2 Motivational Self System' encompasses orientations that some still call 'integrative' and 'instrumental' but which are now theorised in relation to self and identity – aspirations towards particular kinds of linguistico-cultural identity, towards particular capacities to make use of languages for given goals, and so on.

Some concluding remarks

It is generally accepted that learning a second language can be a fairly tough challenge, the demands of which no one is likely to take on willingly unless he/she wants or needs to. Research into second language attitudes and motivation attempts to get to grips with the nature and strength of the wants and needs in question and their sources. This is a vastly complex area and very difficult to investigate, not least because nothing about attitudes and motivation is directly observable. Like love, they are detectable only by their effects ... which are always susceptible to different interpretations.

The notion that feeling good about a language and culture is a good predictor of success in learning the language in question is widespread and to an extent seems to be supported by research. On the other hand we have seen that success may sometimes be interpreted as learning enough of a language to pass a matriculation examination; such success may apparently be won simply on the basis of a consciousness of the vital importance of the examination in question. There are obviously also cases where want and need conspire, as in the case of immigrants who may be enchanted by all aspects of their new surroundings, but who are very aware that without a command of the language of the host country they will find it difficult to get a job.

The recent emphasis on the self in this context is timely, although one assumes that it has always been an unspoken dimension of research in this area. Making it an explicit part of the discussion – the way individuals think about themselves, aspire about themselves, idealise about themselves, accept obligations about themselves, and so on – renders research more difficult but more real. The whole concept of self is impossibly difficult to 'nail down' and the individual variation in this area in limitless, but people's language wants and needs (and the effects of such wants and needs) certainly require to be connected to the vision they have of themselves in relation to the languages in question.

Possible selves   Box 6.15

Possible selves are the ideal selves that we would very much like to become. They are also the selves we could become, and the selves we are afraid of becoming. The possible selves that are hoped for might include the successful self, the creative self, the rich self, the thin self, or the loved and admired self, whereas the dreaded possible selves could be the alone self, the depressed self, the incompetent self, the alcoholic self, the unemployed self, or the bag lady self. (Markus and Nurius 1986)[55]

Postscript   Box 6.16

What do you think the implications of research into motivation and attitudes are for:

- individual students studying in school classrooms?
- individual adult immigrants to a country?
- language teachers?
- parents of school children?
- language teaching methodology in general?
- the teaching of second languages in universities?
- national curricula for language teaching?

Further reading

An excellent introduction to research into attitudes and motivation, covering both theory and practice, this is the completely revised version of a book which Dörnyei published many years ago:

Dörnyei, Z. and Ushioda, E. (2011) *Teaching and Researching Motivation*, 2nd edition. Harlow: Longman.

Dörnyei and Ushioda were also responsible for editing a collection of articles focusing on the link between motivation, self and identity, written by leading scholars from around the world:

Dörnyei, Z. and Ushioda, E. (eds) (2009) *Motivation, Language Identity and the L2 Self*. Bristol: Multilingual Matters.

A recent comprehensive overview and defence of the socio-educational perspective on second language research in the attitudes and research area is:

Gardner, R.C. (2010) *Motivation and Second Language Acquisition: The Socio-Educational Model*. New York: Peter Lang.

An interesting set of perspectives on the pedagogical dimension of attitudes and motivation is to be found in:

Toudic, D. and Mackiewicz, W. (2011) *Handbook on Good Practice that Serves to Motivate Language Learners*. Berlin: MOLAN Network. Online at: http://www.molan-network.org/docs/molan_handbook_0_0.pdf

Clearly, variation in attitudes and motivation constitutes just one of the ways in which L2 learners differ from one another. Some broader perspectives on this issue are provided by the following titles:

Dörnyei, Z. (2005) *The Psychology of the Language Learner: Individual Differences in Second Language Acquisition*. London: Routledge.

Pawlak M. (ed.) (2012) *New Perspectives on Individual Differences in Language Learning and Teaching*. Heidelberg: Springer.

Roberts, L. and Meyer, A. (eds) (2012) *Individual Differences in Second Language Learning*. Oxford: Wiley-Blackwell.

Robinson P. (2002) *Individual Differences and Instructed Language Learning*. Amsterdam: John Benjamins.

Skehan P. (1989) *Individual Differences in Second-Language Learning* . London: Edward Arnold.

References

1. Gammon, C. (2012) *Here 2 Help Services*, blog, accessed 13 January 2012. http://www.here2helpservices.com/wellbeing/heres-how-i-stopped-smoking.html

2. Gardner, R.C. (1985) *Social Psychology and Second Language Learning: The Role of Attitudes and Motivation*. London: Edward Arnold. Test battery online at: http://publish.uwo.ca/~gardner/docs/englishamtb.pdf

3. Ames, C. and Ames, R. (1989) *Research in Motivation in Education*. San Diego: Academic Press.

4. Berry, J.W. (1980) Acculturation as varieties of adaptation. In A.M. Padilla (ed.) (1980) *Acculturation: Theory, Models and Some New Findings*. Boulder, CO: Westview Press, 9–25.

5. Schumann, J.H. (1978) *The Pidginization Process: A Model for Second Language Acquisition*. Rowley, MA: Newbury House.

6. Schumann, J.H. (1986) Research on the acculturation model for second language acquisition. *Journal of Multilingual and Multicultural Development* 7 (5), 379–392.

7. Gabillon, Z. (2005) L2 learner's beliefs: An overview. *Journal of Language and Learning* 3 (3), 233–260.

8. Csizér, K. and Dörnyei, Z. (2005) The internal structure of language learning motivation and its relationship with language choice and learning effort. *The Modern Language Journal* 89 (1), 19–36.

9. Masgoret, A.M. and Gardner, R.C. (2003) Attitudes, motivation and second language learning: A meta-analysis of studies conducted by Gardner and associates. *Language Learning* 53, 123–163.

10. Castellotti, V. and Moore, D. (2002) *Représentations sociales des langues et enseignement. Etude de référence pour le guide pour le développement de politiques linguistiques-éducatives en Europe*. Strasbourg: Conseil de l'Europe, Conseil pour la coopération culturelle.

11. Ushioda, E. (2005) The role of students' attitudes and motivation in second language learning in online language courses. *CALICO Journal* 23 (1), 49–78.

12. Burstall, C., Jamieson, M., Cohen, S. and Hargreaves, M. (1974) *Primary French in the Balance*. Slough: NFER.

13. Green, P. (1975) *The Language Laboratory in School*. Edinburgh: Oliver & Boyd.

14. Littlewood, W. (1984) *Foreign and Second Language Learning*. Cambridge: Cambridge University Press.

15. Hermann-Brennecke, G. (2013) Attitudes and language learning. In M. Byram and A. Hu (eds) (2013) *Routledge Encyclopedia of Language Teaching and Learning*. Abingdon: Routledge, 59–65.

16. De Saint Léger, D. and Storch, N. (2009) Learners' perceptions and attitudes: Implications for willingness to communicate in an L2 classroom. *System* 37 (2), 269–285.

17. Dörnyei, Z. (2001) New themes and approaches in second language motivation research. *Annual Review of Applied Linguistics* 21, 43–59.

18. Dörnyei, Z. and Ottó, I. (1998) Motivation in action: A process model of L2 motivation. *Working Papers in Applied Linguistics* 4, Thames Valley University London, 43–69.

19. Dörnyei, Z. and Kormos, J. (2000) The role of individual and social variables in oral task performance. *Language Teaching Research* 4 (3), 275–300.

20. Deci, E.L. and Ryan, R.M. (1985) *Intrinsic Motivation and Self-Determination in Human Behaviour*. New York: Plenum.

21. Vallerand, R.J. (1997) Toward a hierarchical model of intrinsic and extrinsic motivation. *Advances in Experimental Social Psychology* 29, 271–360.

22. Gardner, R. (2001) Integrative motivation and second language acquisition. In Z. Dornyei and W. Schmidt (eds) (2001) *Motivation and Second Language Acquisition*. Honolulu: University of Hawai'i, 1–19.

23. Lamb, M. (2004) Integrative motivation in a globalizing world. *System* 32 (1), 3–19.

24. Berwick, R. and Ross, S. (1989) Motivation after matriculation: Are Japanese learners of English still alive after exam hell? *JALT Journal* 11 (2), 193–210.

25. Brown, H.D. (2000) *Principles of Language Learning and Teaching*, 4th edition. Englewood Cliffs, NJ: Prentice-Hall.

26. Crystal, D. (2003) *English as a Global Language*. Cambridge: Cambridge University Press.

27. Ushioda, E. (2006) Language motivation in a reconfigured Europe: Access, identity and autonomy. *Journal of Multilingual and Multicultural Development* 27 (2), 148–161.

28. Oxford, R. and Shearin, J. (1994) Language learning motivation: Expanding the theoretical framework. *Modern Language Journal* 78, 12–28.

29. Gardner, R.C. (2006) The socio-educational model of second language acquisition: A research paradigm. *EUROSLA Yearbook* 6, 237–260.

30. Finegan, E. (1999) *Language: Its Structure and Use*, 3rd edition. New York: Harcourt Brace.

31. An Phríomh-Oifig Staidrimh/Central Statistics Office (2012) *This is Ireland: Highlights from Census 2011*. Dublin: Stationery Office.

32. Crookes, G. and Schmidt, R.W. (1991) Motivation: Re-opening the research agenda. *Language Learning* 41 (4), 469–512.

33. Cook, V. (2008) *Second Language Learning and Language Teaching*, 4th edition. London: Hodder.

34. Ó Laoire, M. (2005) Bilingualism in school settings in Ireland: Perspectives on the Irish L2 curriculum. In J. Cohen, K.T. McAlister, K. Rolstad and J. MacSwan (eds) (2005) *Proceedings of the 4th International Symposium on Bilingualism*. Somerville, MA: Cascadilla Press, 1722–1728.

35. Marshall, M. (2002) Promoting learning. Online at: http://teachers.net/gazette/NOV02/marshall.html. Accessed October 2009.

36. Ushioda, E. (2003) Motivation as a socially mediated process. In D. Little, J. Ridley and E. Ushioda (eds) (2003) *Learner Autonomy in the Foreign Language Classroom: Teacher, Learner, Curriculum and Assessment*. Dublin: Authentik, 90–102.

37. Nitta, R. and Asano, R. (2010) Understanding motivational changes in EFL classrooms. In A.M. Stoke (ed.) (2010) *JALT2009 Conference Proceedings*. Tokyo: JALT, 186–195.

38. Ushioda, E. (2001) Language learning at university: Exploring the role of motivational thinking. In Z. Dörnyei and R. Schmidt (eds) (2001) *Motivation and Second Language Acquisition*. Honolulu: University of Hawai'i Second Language Teaching Curriculum Center, 93–125.

39. Bernaus, M. and Gardner, R.C. (2008) Teacher motivation strategies, student perceptions, student motivation, and English achievement. *The Modern Language Journal* 92 (3), 387–401.

40. Dörnyei, Z. (2002) The motivational basis of language learning tasks. In P. Robinson (ed.) (2002) *Individual Differences in Second Language Acquisition*. Amsterdam: John Benjamins, 137–158.

41. Florez, M.C. and Burt, M. (2001) *Beginning to Work with Adult English Language Learners: Some Considerations.* ERIC Digest. Washington, DC: National Center for ESL Literacy Education. Online at: http://www.cal.org/ncle/digests/

42. Clément, R., Dörnyei, Z. and Noels, K.A. (1994) Motivation, self-confidence, and group cohesion in the foreign language classroom. *Language Learning* 44 (3), 417–448.

43. Moss, D. and Van Duzer, C. (1998) *Project-Based Learning for Adult English Language Learners.* Washington, DC: National Center for ESL Literacy Education.

44. Stoller, F. (2006) Establishing a theoretical foundation for project-based learning. In G.H. Beckett and P. Chamness Miller (eds) (2006) *Project-Based Second and Foreign Language Education: Past, Present, and Future.* Charlotte, NC: Information Age Publishing, 19–40.

45. Noels, K.A., Clément, R. and Pelletier, L.G. (2003) Perceptions of teachers' communicative style and students' intrinsic and extrinsic motivation. *Modern Language Journal* 83 (1), 23–34.

46. Ushioda, E. (1997) The role of motivational thinking in autonomous language learning. In D. Little and B. Voss (eds) (1997) *Language Centres: Planning for the New Millennium.* Plymouth: University of Plymouth, CERCLES, Centre for Modern Languages, 39–50.

47. Nakata, Y. (2006) *Motivation and Experience in Foreign Language Learning.* Oxford: Peter Lang.

48. Dörnyei, Z. (2005) *The Psychology of the Language Learner: Individual Differences in Second Language Acquisition.* London: Routledge.

49. Noels, K.S., Pelletier, L.G., Clément, R. and Vallerand, R.J. (2000) Why are you learning a second language? Motivational orientations and self-determination theory. *Language Learning* 50 (1), 57–85.

50. Ushioda, E. and Dörnyei, Z. (2012) Motivation. In S. Gass and A. Mackey (eds) (2012) *The Routledge Handbook of Second Language Acquisition.* New York: Routledge, 396–409.

51. Dörnyei, Z. (2009) *The Psychology of Second Language Acquisition.* Oxford: Oxford University Press.

52. Ushioda, E. (2009) A person-in-context relational view of emergent motivation, self and identity. In Z. Dörnyei and E. Ushioda (eds) (2009) *Motivation, Language Identity and the L2 Self.* Bristol: Multilingual Matters, 215–228.

53. Dörnyei, Z., Csizér, K. and Németh, N. (2006) *Motivation, Language Attitudes and Globalisation: A Hungarian Perspective.* Clevedon: Multilingual Matters.

54. Ushioda, E. (2011) Motivating learners to speak as themselves. In G. Murray, X. Gao and T. Lamb (eds) (2011) *Identity, Motivation and Autonomy in Language Learning.* Bristol: Multilingual Matters, 11–24.

55. Markus, H.R. and Nurius, P. (1986) Possible selves. *American Psychologist* 41, 954–969.

7

How Useful is Second Language Acquisition Research for Language Teaching?

David Singleton

Starter   Box 7.1

How were you taught a second language at school?

(1)   Did you learn lists of vocabulary?
(2)   Did you listen to the teacher explaining grammatical rules?
(3)   Did you repeat sentences after the teacher or a tape?
(4)   Did you do drills in which you practised a single grammatical structure with
      different words?
(5)   Did you carry out tasks in groups with other students?
(6)   Did you encounter authentic speech or writing produced by native speakers?

If you answered 'Yes' to (1–2), you were taught by a grammar translation method, 'Yes' to (3–4)
by an audiolingual method, 'Yes' to (5–6) by a communicative method. The terms are explained
below. Of course most teachers mix methods so you may well have encountered all of them.

Teaching and learning

When people attempt to justify the amount of effort, time and money that is expended
on SLA research, they usually say something about language teaching, as in say the
introductions by Doughty and Long[1] and Larsen Freeman and Long.[2] Of course, they talk
about second language acquisition as being fascinating in its own right, drawing, as it
does, on a number of different domains of knowledge, such as psychology, linguistics,
sociology, anthropology, psycholinguistics, sociolinguistics, neurolinguistics, education,
even politics. They also tend to mention the important theoretical role of SLA research –
the fact that it provides a good test case for linguists' claims about language universals.
Somewhere in the listing of the benefits of the study of second language acquisition,
however, there is always a reference to its contribution to the enrichment of second
language teaching.

Lourdes Ortega has made the modest claim that SLA research can sharpen teaching and
invigorate teachers but she posed some hard questions regarding the extent to which such
research is truly relevant to teachers and teaching.[3] She suggested that its relevance could
emerge under a particular set of conditions, outlined in Box 7.2. However much of the
rest of her talk focused on the proposition that the conditions in question are all too
rarely met. She cited, for example, Belcher's comments that second language researchers
need to[4]:

Research *can* have relevance for teaching   Box 7.2

• when it produces insights in synergy with teacher knowledge;
• when the relation between researchers and teachers is truly negotiated in reciprocity;
• when it empowers teachers in areas where their efficacy is low. (Ortega, 2011)[3]

- consider the teaching dimension early in their research plans 'long before the implications are written up';
- conceive of research problems 'as nested in a number of research and real world contexts';
- contemplate 'the needs of an audience that includes those eager to make the most of our field's partial knowledge on Monday morning'.

Alas, to the implicit question 'Is that what normally happens?', the implicit answer was a clear and resounding 'NO'.

Another approach to this issue might be to look at the kinds of language teaching methodologies that have been in use in the recent (and not so recent) past and to try to discover the extent to which such methodologies have owed any kind of debt to research in general, and to SLA research in particular. David Wilkins divides language teaching methodologies into *traditionalist* and *modernist* approaches.[5] In traditionalist methods, proficient users of language are assumed to possess knowledge about the facts and rules of language, so that the task of language teaching is to find effective ways of transmitting such knowledge to learners. As far as modernist methods are concerned, Wilkins says that they assume that it is not so much conscious knowledge of facts and rules that lies at the heart of the success of language learning as the quality of the linguistic experience that the learner undergoes.

Inductive and deductive language teaching   Box 7.3

Traditionalist teaching tends to conclude that the existence of systematic knowledge about the language system requires that conscious attention should be given to the rules and that these rules should be mastered prior to the attempt to apply them. Such methods are therefore often referred to as *deductive* .... In most modernist teaching ... little importance is attached to the role of conscious learning in this process. Such approaches are therefore often called *inductive*. (Wilkins, 1990)[5]

On this definition, the 'grammar translation method', which both the authors of this book underwent in their foreign language classes, can be labelled 'traditionalist', revolving as it does around 'the explicit study of grammar rules, followed by the completion of grammar exercises and the translation of sentences illustrating particular grammar points, to and from the foreign language'.[6] On the other hand, teaching labelled 'audiolingual' or 'audio-visual', based on courses devised in the period stretching from the 1940s until the 1970s, can be designated as 'modernist', frowning on the explicit study of grammar and promoting the notion that 'grammar and pronunciation were to be learned by habit formation, through intensive oral repetition and pattern practice'.[6]

An example of grammatical explanation   Box 7.4

A preposition is a word that shows certain relations between other words – *in, on, for, with, of, at, to, from* and so on. A preposition is usually a couple of letters long. Here are some examples in Italian: *Di dove sei?* (Where are you from?) *Vado a Pisa* (I am going to Pisa). (Danesi, 2005)[7]

The following sections look closely at the above methodological practices and proposals, and try to come to some conclusions regarding how much they owe to SLA research.

Basically, our conclusion will be that such research has been drawn on less than one might have expected, and that, as Ortega argues,[3] in the future teachers should rightly look for a greater integration of such research with the concerns of language teachers.

The classical method   Box 7.5

Latin was taught by means of what has been called the Classical Method: focus on grammatical rules, memorization of vocabulary and of various declensions and conjugations, translation of texts, doing written exercises ... As other languages began to be taught in educational institutions in the eighteenth and nineteenth centuries, the Classical Method was adopted as the chief means for teaching foreign languages. (Mondal, 2012)[8]

The grammar translation method

The grammar translation method essentially applied the same approach to living languages that had been used in the teaching of 'the classics' in Europe, that is to say, the dead languages, Latin and Ancient Greek. That is why it sometimes goes under the name of the 'classical method'. In the teaching of modern languages as in the teaching of ancient languages, much emphasis was laid on the conscious memorisation of grammatical paradigms and rules, as well as lexical items and expressions, and these memorised elements were then practised by the learners largely by their translating of sentences and (later) longer passages (almost invariably in writing) into and out of the target language. The primary goal of the approach, in English and French as much as in Latin and Ancient Greek, was to give learners access to the literary treasures of the language. A very typical dimension of the grammar translation method was to give the learners lists of words and paradigms to memorise together with their L1 equivalents. Such an approach might be thought to have a naturalness deficit, to lack 'ecological validity'. It is worth remembering, however (see also Topic 2), that, in both first and second language acquisition, speech directed at novice acquirers is often characterised by the use of ostensive definition (giving the meaning by pointing to the object 'That's a hippopotamus') – which is isolating and explicit – and that rehearsal (repeating things over to yourself) is a feature of the way in which both first language and second language acquirers spontaneously come to grips with new forms.

In fact, the way in which the grammar translation method has just been characterized is over-simplified. A typical pedagogical unit taught within this framework usually began with an introductory passage in the target language for reading and translation, followed by a list of the new words introduced in the passage together with their translation glosses into the learners' mother tongue. Then came some explanations of the grammatical points exemplified in the passage, some related grammatical exercises and some exercises involving translation into and out of the target language. This was not necessarily the end, though. The final part of the unit often consisted of supplementary activities such as the learning of poems, songs, etc. in the target language. For example, a simple (and undistinguished) six-line poem 'Herbstleid' ('Autumn song') by J.G. von Salis-Seewis appears early in the introductory German textbook for evening-class students, *Heute Abend!*[9]

Clearly, the vocabulary lists and grammar points provided the basis for conscious memorisation (a typical homework exercise). Opportunities for inductive learning, however, were also provided – by the text which opened the unit, by the second language instructions and examples associated with the exercises, by the meaningful contexts within the grammar exercises and indeed by the translation tasks. In striving to render first language texts accurately into the target language, learners would have been very likely to retain some of the expressions they deployed, even in the absence of any attempt at conscious memorisation. It is also worth noting that the literary preoccupations of the grammar translation approach meant that learners were not only presented with poems, songs, etc., in language classes but that more advanced learners were also, as they progressed, expected to read and study entire literary works – in class but also in their own time. Obviously, such extensive reading accompanied by study was likely to occasion the picking up of new material on the basis of encountering it and analysing it in context.

All in all, we can say that the grammar translation approach was not just about the conscious memorisation and practice of rules and lexical items. It also supplied plenty of opportunities for unconscious, inductive acquisition from context. The great drawback of this method was that it tended to be taught largely through the medium of the learners' first language, which meant that exposure to the target language was largely limited to the processing of texts and exercises. Another aspect of this limitation was that the target language input received by learners was principally in the written medium, which obviously restricted their chances of becoming fully familiar with the phonological shapes of words and structures.

We come now to the question of how much the grammar translation method owed to SLA research. The short answer to this question is that it owed nothing at all to second language research – or to research of any kind. This approach essentially goes back to ancient times. For example, the quotation in Box 7.6 describes the teaching of Greek in the Roman Empire – hundreds of years before the advent of second language research and educational research in general. This classical method was the fruit of what was seen as common sense, as well as of experience. The fact that the method survived is some kind of testimony to its success. At least within the confines of its specific aims, it appears to have succeeded. Thanks to the classical method, Cicero undoubtedly learned to read Plato in Rome in the 1st century BC, and at least some English schoolchildren of the 1960s learned to read Livy, Racine and Goethe in Latin, French and German. On some of the particularities of the approach we shall have more to say later.

Classical teaching   Box 7.6

[G]rammar was viewed as the way to read classical texts ... Word by word, heavily supported by interlinear and/or marginal glosses ... and parallel translation ..., students read edifying passages and single sentences from classical literature ... and memorized sayings, metaphors and adages ... (Fotos, 2005)[10]

Summary: The grammar translation (GT) method   Box 7.7

Universally popular in schools until the 1950s, still much used in universities.

Aim: to appreciate the L2 literature, to understand its grammar and to enhance thinking.

Signature techniques:
- explaining grammatical rules and structures to students;
- working closely on translations of written texts;
- memorising lists of vocabulary.

Learning implications:
- conscious study of grammar leads to its acquisition;
- L2 learning depends on links to the L1 already known;
- vocabulary can be learnt by rote.

The audiolingual method

The audiolingual method started life as the 'army method', an approach developed in the USA in the latter years of the Second World War to prepare American military personnel for duties in mainland Europe after D-Day. It was created not by university language teaching professors focused on the great literature of France, Germany, etc., but by structuralist linguists, who were heavily influenced by behaviourist psychology. American structuralist linguistics at the time, under the tutelage of Leonard Bloomfield, was particularly interested in physical things that could be observed (phonology, morphology and syntax) rather than the study of 'invisible' meaning.[11] As for behaviourist psychology, it viewed language acquisition in terms of habit formation – the selective reinforcement of particular responses to particular stimuli in particular conditions (as in animal training).[12,13,14]

Unsurprisingly, then, the methodology that emerged focused especially on the manipulation of form. It was based on imitation and highly repetitive drilling of formal structures, summed up by Wilga Rivers as 'mimicry-memorization (usually of dialogue material) and pattern drilling (whereby students learn to manipulate structures to a point of automatic response to a language stimulus)'.[15] After the Second World War, this methodology became known as 'audiolingualism'. It was paralleled in Europe by the 'audio-visual' method, which had similar basic assumptions but additionally emphasised the creation of meaning in the students' minds through the association of pictures and sentences. A typical unit of an audio-visual course would open with a filmstrip accompanied by an audio-recorded dialogue, the students repeating the dialogue frame by frame. The dialogue would then be followed by a series of exercises in which the learners would practise forms and constructions included in the dialogue. The unit would usually also have associated with it a battery of structure drills intended for use in a language laboratory. It was this methodology that prompted the development of language laboratories and their widespread acquisition by educational institutions[16] and indeed the practice in much commercial material available for use on computers.

Opportunities for inductive learning from context were obviously presented by the dialogues and the accompanying visual aids. The dialogue told a story, which was usually linked to a larger narrative theme running through the entire course. While the stories in question hardly constituted high drama, they probably contained enough of interest to motivate attention to their meaning – despite the meaning-shyness of the originators of the approach! As in the case of the grammar translation method, further potential learning opportunities were provided by the exercises associated with the lesson – both those orchestrated by the teacher immediately after the dialogues and the further structure drills performed later in the language laboratory.

Finally all audiolingual teaching had to proceed entirely in the target language, sharply contrasting with the use of the first language in the grammar translation method. This meant that, quite apart from the material in the dialogues and exercises, learners received additional second language input from the teacher – in the form of commentaries on the dialogue, explanations relating to activities, instructions having to do with classroom management, etc. Obviously, learners needed to attend closely to such input in order to keep abreast of what was happening and what they were supposed to be doing. In the process they would have undoubtedly acquired some of the material that recurred in such classroom discourse. And the final phase of the cycle, in principle although not always in practice, was the students assimilating the language taught into their own speech through extension activities.

Decontextualised language learning was not supposed to figure in audiolingual methodology, but, as with the grammar translation method, the stereotypical image of the approach was not always adhered to. Some audiolingually inspired teachers' manuals did contain

---

An American example of a structure drill, alias pattern practice   Box 7.8

What is he reading?	He's reading a book.
What is she reading?	She's reading a book.
What are they reading?	They're reading a book.
What are you reading?	I'm reading a book.
What is he writing?	He's writing some letters.

... (Lado and Fries, 1958)[17]

A British example

My son's hoping to stay in a lively place this time.
Lively? Then the place not to stay is Stoke!
Lady Heston's hoping to go to an exciting place this time.
Exciting? Then the place not to go to is Stoke!
Charles is hoping to move to an interesting place this time.
Interesting? Then the place not to move to is Stoke!
... (Abbs, Cook and Underwood, 1970)[18]

instructions regarding the treatment of particular vocabulary and morphology.[19] Some audio-visual courses indeed used 'Visual Grammar', a technique for explaining grammar with visual codes, such as a cross superimposed on a picture for negation and speech bubbles referring to the future being one colour, those referring to the past another. The teaching recommended in such cases certainly related to the context of the dialogues, but specific items were mentioned as requiring attention. Many of the other activities proposed under the heading of 'practice' also had a quasi-isolating dimension – structure drills involving repeated focus on specific lexical elements, different forms of particular verbs or nouns, grammatical gender, etc. (see Box 7.8).

It is not unreasonable to conclude that the audiolingual approach offered not only plenty of scope for inductive, contextualised acquisition but also some more focused opportunities for laying down memory traces for new material. Audiolingual methodology worked hand in glove with Contrastive Analysis – the idea that learners' mistakes could be anticipated by comparing the structures of the two languages – which basically saw interference from the mother tongue as the principal bane of the L2 user's life. Accordingly audiolingual teaching banned all use of the first language from the second language classroom and did not encourage the making of semantic-associative links between second language and first language expressions. Given all we know, however, about the interconnectedness of the mental lexicons of the first and second languages (see Topics 1 and 4), such links were undoubtedly forged anyway.

Alas, though, the absence of any possibility, according to audiolingual orthodoxy, of giving learners the first language equivalents of the newly introduced material through translation sometimes led to misunderstandings regarding their meanings. On one occasion, for example, a group of learners of English in Africa, having had the word *turkey* explained to them by their teacher in English, went away thinking that the expression in question meant 'ostrich'. Nor did pictures necessarily solve the problem. On another occasion, an English learner of French, misled by a not very well drawn visual aid, spent a considerable period of time under the impression that the French word *carnet* ('notebook') meant 'candy-bar'.

Another drawback of the approach was that the range of vocabulary it made available tended to be somewhat limited, often being based only on high frequency words, which tended to render audiolingual materials somewhat bland, with little of the savour of real-life conversations. A further disadvantage associated with audiolingualism was its emphasis on oral-aural aspects of the target language to the point where written language was often totally excluded until relatively late in the teaching programme. Since the learners in question were typically habituated to taking written notes in their other school subjects, this tended to lead to the invention of the learners' own (usually highly idiosyncratic) system of transcribing the second language. This in turn meant that the orthographic entries they had for target language words in their mental lexicons often bore little resemblance to the standard spellings of these words. Denying learners access to literacy skills in the L2 over a substantial length of time also deprived learners of the opportunity to acquire or support target language elements from reading.

We return to our $64 question: how much was this teaching approach influenced by SLA research? It was certainly influenced by psychological ideas about language acquisition, namely behaviourism. Such ideas were not at all based on any kind of investigation into second language acquisition, nor indeed first language acquisition. Rather they flowed from the behaviourist claim, based on the observation and training of animals in laboratories, that all learning is a matter of habit formation – conditioning. This was largely challenged by Chomsky's celebrated review of B.F. Skinner's book *Verbal Behavior*[20] in 1959, which set linguistics against behaviourism for 20 years and led to much direct investigation of children's language.

The linguistics input into audiolingualism was based on the axioms and practices of Bloomfieldian structuralism, the dominant approach in linguistics prior to Chomsky, and had no connection with issues of language acquisition. This is not to say that audiolingualism ran counter to almost everything that has emerged from second language research since the 1960s. Thus, for example, the importance of imitation, much beloved of audiolingualism, is now beginning to be re-emphasised in SLA research circles, for example in Chappell.[21]

Though these two teaching methods are seldom found in a pure form in a 21st century classroom, they represent two opposite poles of thinking about teaching and about language that are still highly relevant today. On the one hand the grammar translation method depends on people understanding some aspects of the language consciously and on working with the meaning of texts in the second language and how they can be related to the meanings in the first language through translation. On the other the audiolingual method depended on people acquiring the language as if it were a physical skill without conscious understanding of the language and with a minimal reliance on meaning. Both of them were far richer in practice than the sterile images that come across from books on teaching methodology. And obviously they worked: vast numbers of students successfully acquired the language through both methods.

The communicative approach

Let us look finally at the communicative approach, now well-established after 30 years of use and having many modern variants. Interestingly, at least in some of its manifestations, communicative teaching combines elements of the traditionalist and modernist approaches outlined by Wilkins.[5] The original motivation for the development of communicative language teaching in the 1970s related to the fact that large numbers of members of the European workforce were migrating to other European countries to find employment. The concern was to equip such migrants with linguistic skills which would enable them to meet their professional and personal requirements in countries and languages other than their own. This situation generated a set of ideas relating to the analysis of learners' communicative needs in terms of the functions of language and the notions expressed through language, the definition of course objectives in terms of the meanings that related to such needs, the early exposure of learners to authentic samples of the target language, and the development of pedagogical activities which had clear relevance to real-life needs. In other words, the communicative movement sought to connect language teaching and learning in the classroom as transparently as possible to learners' likely uses of the target language.

Summary: The audiolingual method   Box 7.9

Popular in schools from the 1950s to the 1970s, mostly American in origin.

Aim: to use the language rather than to know it consciously.

Signature techniques:
- structure drills in which the same grammatical structure is repetitively practised with variations of vocabulary;
- dialogues in which a short recorded dialogue is repeated several times by the students, sentence by sentence.

Learning implications:
- unconscious practice of structures leads to their acquisition;
- L2 learning depends on creating automatic habits for using the language;
- vocabulary can be learnt by rote;
- L2 learning proceeds independently of the L1 in the students' minds.

When such ideas were applied in primary and secondary schools, a broader view had to be taken of students' needs, since it was not clear to most school pupils what their real-life needs in a second language might be. Accordingly, the notion of needs was more broadly defined, in its new incarnation encompassing interests and expectations. Also, attention began to be paid to the needs of learners relative to life within the actual language classroom. Despite such adjustments, the essential features of the communicative approach remained:

- a commitment to founding second language teaching programmes on an analysis of what the learner needed, wanted or expected to be able to do with the second language in question;
- acceptance of the proposition that it is principally through experience of the meaning-mediating dimension of language that language acquisition progresses.

However, different versions of communicative language teaching nevertheless take different positions on issues like the use of the learners' first language, 'focus on form' (i.e. overt discussion of grammar), and the ways in which the course objectives are presented. In all its variety, communicative language teaching remains the pedagogical paradigm with most influence in much of the world. In the 1990s it was being said that the communicative approach was well established as the 'dominant theoretical model' in language teaching,[22] and more recent publications continue, implicitly and explicitly, to reiterate that same message, such as Duff,[23] Murray[24] and Richards.[25]

Examples of communicative exercises   Box 7.10

Student A, choose one of the jobs or places on page 16. This is your job. Write a sentence.
Student B, guess A's sentence.[26]

1   You are the shop assistant in a local store. Look at the information and serve the customer:
    Prices. . . . .
2   Go to the local store and try to buy these things some stamps some toothpaste . . .
    (Cunningham and Moor, 2005)[27]

One could hardly accuse communicative language teaching of denying learners the opportunity to acquire language inductively from context. Communicative programmes in all their forms are extremely rich in learner-oriented reading, listening and viewing material. Much of this is 'authentic' in the technical sense of having originally been produced to entertain or inform the target language community. Much of it is also in one way or another nowadays supported by computer-assisted interactive dimensions. Other opportunities for inductive learning are furnished by exercises in the target language – also often associated in various ways with authenticity and interactivity. In addition, while some versions of communicative language teaching allow for some use of the learners' mother tongue in class, the normal understanding is that, as far as is practicable, the target language should be used as the medium of instruction. As in the case of the audiolingual approach, this implies many further opportunities for inductive learning.

Communicative teaching and grammar translation   Box 7.11

Communicative methodology has become so eclectic that it will adopt almost any technique that furthers the students' ability to communicate … It is not the individual features … that are exclusive, it is the overall pattern of how different techniques that may be common in both approaches are used in proportion to each other. The communicative teacher, for example, may on occasion go over the rules of grammar or deal with translation, without necessarily being accused of deserting the communicative camp. This does not mean that there is no 'specific' difference between the CA and the grammar translation method, rather that they may use similar techniques but in different proportions and combinations. (Harbord, 2003)[28]

With regard to opportunities for language item and pattern learning of a more deliberative kind, many varieties of communicative language teaching incorporate such a focus to a greater or lesser extent. Indeed in a book I co-authored some years ago on the use of authentic materials, conceived within the communicative framework,[29] an entire chapter is devoted to 'Using authentic texts to develop learners' conscious control of the target language'. Exercises proposed in this chapter – which are very much in tune with the kinds of exercises one finds in a wide range of communicative materials – include relating expressions in particular texts to their semantic fields and collocation possibilities.

Clearly, such exercises concentrate the learner's mind on the meaning and usage of specific items. A further exercise-type juxtaposes second language words with first language descriptions of aspects of their meaning. Far from being out of keeping with the spirit of the communicative approach by referring to the learners' mother tongue, such an exercise picks up on some of the earliest and founding texts of communicative language teaching, some of which actually advocated the rehabilitation of translation (for example, see Henry Widdowson's remarks in Box 7.12).

Usefulness of translation   Box 7.12

I want to argue that translation, conceived of in a certain way, can be a very useful pedagogic device and indeed in some circumstances, notably those where a foreign language is being learned for 'special purposes' as a service subject, translation of a kind may provide the most effective means of learning. (Widdowson, 1979)[30]

There is obviously much to be said in favour of the communicative approach. There is a sense in which the 'communicative approach' escapes Wilkins' definitions of traditionalist and modernist. At least in some of its versions exemplified above, it seems to combine the advantages of the grammar translation method (rich input, association between target language and mother tongue forms, explicit focus on the profile of linguistic units, availability of written forms) with the advantages of the audiolingual method (classroom discourse in the target language, visual support, provision of substantial oral-aural input). Furthermore, it aspires to address learners' needs, interests and expectations in a way that the other two methods do not, and thus in principle ought to deliver teaching and learning materials which have more personal significance for learners than what is delivered by the other methods.

That is not to say, however, that everything in the garden is rosy so far as the communicative approach is concerned. For example, communicative materials have not always been as attentive as they might have been in encouraging the rehearsal of new target material. Also, some of the authentic material by which the communicative approach sets such store dates extremely rapidly, which may, if such material is included in textbooks, undermine the claim of communicative language teaching to be in touch with learners' needs in using the target language in the 'real world'.

As for the debt of the communicative approach to SLA research, once again, to look for such a debt is to court disappointment. The primary sources of research influence on the early communicativists were a branch of linguistic ethnography and a branch of linguistic philosophy. From the former, in the person of Dell Hymes, came the notion of 'communicative competence', a radical broadening of the Chomskyan concept of competence 'to account for the fact that a normal child acquires knowledge of sentences not only as grammatical, but also as appropriate ... acquires competence as to when to speak, when not, and as to what to talk about with whom, when, where, in what manner'.[31] From the latter came the idea – originating with J.L. Austin[32] and further elaborated by John Searle[33] – that all linguistic communication events are acts, 'speech acts', more properly 'language acts': speaking is doing. This conception underlay the communicative 'functions' of functional-notional syllabuses.[34] Neither of the two sources mentioned above is affiliated specifically to SLA research.

Various aspects of SLA research have certainly fed into the communicative enterprise. For example, the importance attached to large quantities of comprehensible input in the 1980s can be related to Stephen Krashen's advocacy of this view.[35] Also the benefits of linking pedagogical material to the learner's own world and aspirations might be linked to recent work on attitudes and motivation, as discussed in Topic 6. It is difficult to argue this point too strongly though. After all, exposure to extensive input has always been recognised as having a useful role in language learning, as its centuries-old role in the grammar translation approach testifies. As for the acknowledgment that paying attention to the learner's inner universe of interests and needs would improve the attitudinal and motivational underpinnings of learning, this could be regarded as part of the unspoken folk wisdom of teaching, to which good teachers have always attended. In any case, such ideas are certainly not confined to ideas emerging from the SLA research domain.

Summary: The communicative approach   Box 7.13

Popular globally from the 1970s onwards, shading recently into task-based learning, mostly British in origin.

Aim: people communicating to each other both outside and inside the classroom.

Signature elements:
- the use of authentic spoken and written texts;
- tasks in which students have to cooperate to produce a particular outcome;
- relating the language the student is taught to their communicative needs.

Learning implications:
- second languages are acquired by communicating in them;
- learners should be exposed to 'real' examples of native speaker communication;
- tasks in the classroom should be constructed around communication and interaction.

Some concluding remarks

As was remarked at the outset of this chapter, SLA research often justifies itself in terms of the benefits it brings to the teaching of additional languages. Teachers, accordingly, often have very high expectations about what SLA research can contribute – excessively high expectations one might say. We should perhaps never forget that this area of research got under way only half a century ago – as compared, for example, to the study of grammar, which has been with us for thousands of years – and also that many of its founders wanted to remove such research from the realm of instructed learning to that of 'naturalistic' instruction.

While such SLA research does reveal to an extent what L2 learners do and what they know at various stages under various conditions, it cannot yet provide a detailed itinerary of the processes which lead to such behaviour and knowledge. Also, while it is true that such research has demonstrated the inevitability (and possible usefulness) of such traditional teacher irritants as 'error' and cross-linguistic influence, it is far from being able to advise teachers what precisely their stance should be on these issues. Still less are the results of SLA research directly translatable into a pedagogical recipe book.

SLA research is then valuable as an instrument for promoting greater teacher awareness of various aspects of the acquisition process and greater sensitivity towards learners. It may also be the case that learners who have looked into this kind of research can draw on their awareness of the second language acquisition process to facilitate their learning, as we see in Kathy Rich's fascinating account of her learning of Hindi.[36] We need to concede, though, that Ortega is probably right in suggesting that, before SLA research can aspire to contribute usefully and meaningfully to the development of language teaching methodology, it will need to embed itself with much more will and enthusiasm in the everyday realities of the language classroom.

Postscript   Box 7.14

How would you now prefer to be taught a new language? Put these in order of preference:

- communicating in groups in the classroom;
- dealing with literary texts;
- learning words by heart;
- having grammatical rules explained to you;
- repeating words or phrases;
- hearing and reading authentic native language;
- practising structure drills.

Which of these is true of your experience of language instruction on the computer?

Further reading

The following two books provide a solid and comprehensive treatment of second language teaching:

Larsen-Freeman, D. (2000) *Techniques and Principles in Language Teaching*, 2nd edition. Oxford: Oxford University Press.

Richards, J.C. and Rodgers, T.S. (2001) *Approaches and Methods in Language Teaching*, 2nd edition. Cambridge: Cambridge University Press.

A brief and readable good start in regard to communicative language teaching is Littlewood's book on the topic, still very useful despite its age:

Littlewood, W. (1981) *Communicative Language Teaching: An Introduction*. Cambridge: Cambridge University Press.

A thoughtful theoretical offering on the concept of 'learning' in the context of language teaching is:

Seedhouse, P., Walsh, S. and Jenks, C. (eds) (2010) *Conceptualising 'Learning' in Applied Linguistics*. Basingstoke: Palgrave Macmillan.

Finally, in our globalised world, collections like the following have a very valuable role, and will be increasingly needed:

Leung, C. and Creese, A. (eds) (2010) *English as an Additional Language: Approaches to Teaching Linguistic Minority Students*. London: Sage.

References

1. Doughty, C.J. and Long, M.H. (2005) The scope of inquiry and goals of SLA. In C.J. Doughty and M.H. Long (eds) (2005) *The Handbook of Second Language Acquisition*. Malden: Blackwell, 1–16.

2. Larsen Freeman, D. and Long, M.H. (1991) *An Introduction to SLA Research*. London: Longman.

3. Ortega, L. (2012) Language acquisition research for language teaching: Choosing between application and relevance. In B. Hinger, E. M. Unterrainer & D. Newby (eds) (2012) *Sprachen lernen: Kompetenzen entwickeln? Performanzen (über)prüfen*. Vienna: Präsens Verlag, 24–38.

4. Belcher, D. (2007) A bridge too far? *TESOL Quarterly* 41 (2), 396–399.

5. Wilkins, D.A. (1990) Second languages: How they are learned and taught. In N.E. Collinge (ed.) (1990) *An Encyclopaedia of Language*, 518–550. London: Routledge.

6. Mitchell, R. (2000) Foreign language education: Balancing communicative needs and intercultural understanding. In M. Ben-Peretz, S. Brown and B. Moon (eds) (2000) *Routledge International Companion to Education*, 921–934. London: Routledge.

7. Danesi, M. (2005) *Italian Now*. New York: Barrons.

8. Mondal, N.K. (2012) A comparative study of grammar translation method and communicative approach in teaching English language. *New York Science Journal* 5 (5), 86–93.

9. Kelber, M. (1938) *Heute Abend!* London: Ginn and Company.

10. Fotos, S. (2005) Traditional and grammar translation methods for second language teaching. In E. Hinkel (ed.) (2005) *Handbook of Research in Second Language Teaching and Learning: Volume 1*. London: Routledge, 652–670.

11. Bloomfield, L. (1933) *Language*. New York: Holt.

12. Skinner, B.F. (1957) *Verbal Behavior*. New York: Appleton-Century-Crofts.

13. Lado, R. (1964) *Language Teaching: A Scientific Approach*. New York: McGraw-Hill.

14. Brooks, N. (1960) *Language and Language Learning*. New York: Harcourt Brace.

15. Rivers, W.M. (1968) *Teaching Foreign-Language Skills*. Chicago, IL: University of Chicago Press.

16. Roby, W.B. (2004) Technology in the service of foreign language learning: The case of the language laboratory. In D.H. Jonassen (ed.) (2004) *Handbook of Research for Educational Communications and Technology*, 2nd edition. Mahwah, NJ; Lawrence Erlbaum, 523–542.

17. Lado, R. and Fries C.C. (1958) *English Pronunciation.* Ann Arbor: University of Michigan Press.

18. Abbs, B., Cook, V. and Underwood, M. (1968) *Realistic English.* Oxford: Oxford University Press.

19. Moget, M-T. and Boudot, J. (1972) *De Vive Voix.* Paris: Didier.

20. Chomsky, N. (1959) Review of B.F. Skinner *Verbal Behavior. Language* 35, 26–58.

21. Chappell, P. (2012) A sociocultural account of the role of imitation in instructed second language learning. *Journal of Linguistics and Language Teaching* 3 (1), 61–91.

22. Thompson, G. (1996) Some misconceptions about communicative language teaching. *ELT Journal* 50 (1), 9–15.

23. Duff, P. (2013) Communicative language teaching. In M. Celce-Murcia, D. Brinton and M.A. Snow (eds) *Teaching English as a Second or Foreign Language,* 4th edition. Independence, KY: Heinle Cengage.

24. Murray, N. (2010) *Communicative Language Teaching: Reflections and Implications for Language Teacher Education.* Berlin: VDM Verlag Dr. Müller.

25. Richards, J.C. (2006) *Communicative Language Teaching Today.* Cambridge: Cambridge University Press.

26. Doff, A. (2010) *English Unlimited.* Cambridge: Cambridge University Press.

27. Cunningham, S. and Moor, P. (2005) *New Cutting Edge.* Harlow: Pearson Longman.

28. Harbord, J. (2003) Contribution to: A question of definitions: An investigation through the definitions and practices of communicative and task-based approaches (TESL-EJ Forum, Karen Stanley, editor). *TESL-EJ* 7 (3), accessed 8 June 2013. Online at: http://tesl-ej.org/ej27/f1.html

29. Little, D., Devitt, S. and Singleton, D. (1994) *Learning Foreign Languages from Authentic Texts: Theory and Practice.* Dublin: Authentik.

30. Widdowson, H.G. (1979) The deep structure of discourse and the use of translation. In C.J. Brumfit and K. Johnson (eds) (1979) *The Communicative Approach to Language Teaching.* Oxford: Oxford University Press, 61–71.

31. Hymes, D. (1972) Models of the interaction of language and social life. In J. J. Gumperz and D. Hymes (eds) (1972) *Directions in Sociolinguistics: The Ethnography of Communication.* New York: Holt, Rinehart & Winston, 35–71.

32. Austin, J.L. (1962) *How to Do Things with Words.* Oxford: Clarendon Press.

33. Searle, J.R. (1969) *Speech Acts: An Essay in the Philosophy of Language.* Cambridge: Cambridge University Press.

34. Singleton, D. (1994) Defending notional-functional syllabuses. In C. Brumfit (ed.) (1994) *The Work of the Council of Europe and Second Language Teaching.* London: Macmillan, 75–80.

35. Krashen, S.D. (1982) *Principles and Practice in Second Language Acquisition.* Oxford: Pergamon.

36. Rich, K. (2010) *Dreaming in Hindi: Life in Translation.* London: Portobello Books.

8

What are the Goals of Language Teaching?

Vivian Cook

Starter: Why learn another language? Box 8.1

Circle the answers you agree with.

(1) Language learning helps you to get a job.
      Strongly agree **a** **b** **c** **d** **e** *strongly disagree*
(2) Language learning helps you to develop other skills.
      Strongly agree **a** **b** **c** **d** **e** *strongly disagree*
(3) Language learning provides better opportunities to travel abroad.
      Strongly agree **a** **b** **c** **d** **e** *strongly disagree*
(4) Language learning is enjoyable.
      Strongly agree **a** **b** **c** **d** **e** *strongly disagree*

Taken from *Seven Hundred Reasons for Studying Languages*[1]

So why would anyone want to learn another language? What goal do the learners themselves have in mind and what goals do others lay down for them? This chapter looks at the types of outcome people want from L2 learning. It differs from Topic 6 in looking at where the learners want to get to rather than the different means for getting there.

Like human beings in general, people who use a second language, L2 users, come in all shapes and sizes, races and creeds and can be divided up in many ways. In other words there are many possible goals in language learning, amounting to a choice of which kind of L2 user you want to be.

The hierarchy of languages

De Swaan's hierarchy of languages Box 8.2

Hyper-central languages	English
Super-central languages	French, Arabic, Spanish
Central languages	Italian
Local (peripheral languages)	Finnish, Welsh

Abram de Swaan classifies languages into four groups.[2] One group is languages spoken within a limited geographical area, say one country or a part of one country, called *peripheral* or *local* languages. People do not usually learn local languages as second languages except for those who migrate into the relevant area. One such language is Finnish, hardly spoken outside Finland and parts of Sweden. Another is Welsh, confined to Wales apart from a pocket of speakers in Argentina. Some local languages, however, span several countries, thanks to the arbitrary modern borders between some countries. Kurdish is a native language in Iraq, Turkey and Iran; Kazakh in Kazakhstan, China and Uzbekistan; Romani in Poland, Serbia, Hungary, Romania and many other countries. Historically it was only in the 18th century that languages came to be seen as the crucial identifying aspect of a country. England after all was governed for centuries by kings and queens who were native speakers of French, German and Dutch.

A second group of languages is the main language within each country, called *central* languages. Speakers of local languages other than the central language have to learn them to live. Italian is the central language for Italy and so is used by the Italians who speak German, Ladino, Sardinian, Venetian and other languages.

Next comes a group of *super-central* languages, which are used for certain functions across several countries. French is an official language across a band of African countries such as the Cameroon, Burkina Faso, Mali and others. It is still a language of diplomacy and an official language of the Olympic Games, even if it was hardly visible at London 2012. These super-central languages are often taught as foreign languages in schools in other countries, say French, German or Spanish.

Finally comes the only *hyper-central* language, English. This is spoken in almost any country for any purpose and is now taught in most countries of the world. One estimate from the British Council is that there are two billion learners of English (which still of course means only two in seven of the world's population). English has a unique status. It has become a global lingua franca, not just for communicating with native speakers, but also predominantly for communication with non-native speakers, for good or for ill. According to David Graddol, rather than schools teaching the three Rs – reading, writing and arithmetic – English is now the 4th R in primary education, taken for granted as a useful tool for children to have rather than 'just' a second language.[3]

Groups of L2 users

Let us start by looking at six broad groups of L2 users that relate in part to De Swaan's four types of language.[4]

(1) *People who are part of multilingual communities.* In many parts of the world, people now live in communities where several languages are spoken, as the notice outside the Newcastle Civic Centre in Figure 8.1 shows. Newcastle upon Tyne in the North of England is home to people who speak Cantonese, British Sign Language, African French, Romani and many others. The notice shows that some concession has been made to their diverse language needs. As well as visiting the civic centre, most of them need English for dealing with their banks, their employers, public transport and all the other basic necessities for living in a city.

So people who live in multilingual societies – and in a sense who doesn't these days? – need a central language to interact not only with the people who speak it but also with people from other linguistic backgrounds, whether local languages or languages of migrants. As a central language, Mandarin Chinese can enable speakers of the seven Chinese languages in China (known confusingly as dialects) to communicate with each other in speech and in

Figure 8.1 *Newcastle upon Tyne Civic Centre*

the common written language. Portuguese in Brazil has a similar unifying function for the speakers of the 215 languages in Brazil, as well as its super-central role for communicating with the other Portuguese-speaking countries in Europe and Africa. For many people the ability to use another language alongside their own is vital to their lives in their own home countries. Children who grow up speaking another language than the central language of their environment need to acquire it to function outside their parents' home.

(2) *People regaining their cultural heritage.* Recent years have increasingly seen people travel around the world. One British Indian undergraduate told me she was going to spend her summer visiting an uncle in India and a cousin in New York: her family was all around the globe. Many of the younger generations feel they should make contact with their roots, particularly in terms of language. So some Hispanics in the United States learn Spanish to go back to their ancestral Puerto Rico[5]; pre-school children in a local authority in Scotland are introduced 'to Gaelic as a means of enriching their own cultural identity'.[6] In Newcastle upon Tyne, the Mandarin School has been teaching children Mandarin Chinese on Saturdays for many years, emphasising 'the importance of traditional and contemporary Chinese cultures, so that the pupils have a better understanding of the language, and how and why it is used'.[7]

In England this goal is called 'community languages', in the USA 'heritage languages'. The point is to learn a language that is culturally identified with your heritage, even if neither your parents nor your ancestors actually spoke it. The Chinese children in Newcastle upon Tyne mostly come from Cantonese-speaking families for whom Mandarin has been a central second language, never a first language. Indeed community languages have come back from near-death for cultural and political reasons, like Hebrew in Israel and Irish in Ireland, the first 20th century generation of speakers of Hebrew being L2 users.

This shades over into the learning of super-central languages for cultural purposes. Often a prestige language is associated with the sacred writings and rituals of a particular religion, say Classical Arabic for Islam and Biblical Hebrew for Judaism. To become a member of these religions, it is necessary for people to have at least some acquaintance with the language in which their main truths and ceremonies are expressed. Until 1965, the same applied to Church Latin for the Catholic church so that Catholics could attend mass in the same language all over the world. Some worldwide pursuits are associated with particular languages. It would be hard to practise judo for example without using such Japanese terms as *ippon* (defeating someone in a single manoeuvre) or *sensei* (teacher). While people may not acquire very much of the second language in such circumstances, it is nevertheless a genuine use of a super-central language and important to their lives.

(3)   *Short-term visitors to another country.* One change in modern life is the extent to which people move around the globe for short stays. Some travel for their jobs, whether businessmen going to meetings, academics going to conferences or tennis players competing in the ATP World Tour. Some go on holiday to destinations that are always getting further away – English people go to Peru, Burma or Tibet where 20 years ago they went to Spain and France and 100 years ago to Bournemouth and Blackpool. Some are overseas students studying on short or long courses in London or Shanghai. Many of these visits involve a second language.

This goes in both directions. The visitors need to communicate with the locals, whether in their hotels or in their supermarkets, even if this involves rather little of a second language. The visited need the language to serve their customers in the tourist, transport and education industries. The second language need not necessarily be the local language: 74% of tourism through English involves only L2 users,[3] say Japanese visiting Cuba or Russians going to Spain. Traditionally tourism has been assumed to be an important aspect of second languages for adults; my hairdresser told me she had enjoyed being able to practise her Spanish in Majorca.

So the functions of the second language vary from the minimal needs of a package holiday in Guardalavaca in Cuba to the demands of a conference in English for a Pole in Sarajevo, not only interacting with other participants but delivering a paper in English. They are mostly, in de Swaan's terms, confined to specialist super-central functions: the second language covers part of life, not all of it. Some Greek students in the UK have refused to learn any English other than that required for their academic courses and books; English serves them solely as a vehicle to a qualification and a job.

(4)   *People using an L2 with partners, friends or children.* Because of increasing cross-cultural contacts, people often have friends or partners who speak another language: Johnny Depp and his former partner Vanessa Paradis spoke English and French respectively; Arnold Schwarzenegger and Maria Shriver spoke German and English;

Aristotle Onassis married Jackie Kennedy, bringing together Greek and English – hopefully it is a coincidence that two of these relationships broke up. Partners in such relationships are very confident about their ability to communicate to each other in the second language, indeed to pass for native speakers.[8] Relationships starting on the internet may be carried out through a common language, without either person realising till they actually meet that one of them can't use the spoken language.

Summary: Groups of L2 users and learners[4]   Box 8.3

L2 users
(1) people who are part of multilingual communities;
(2) people regaining their cultural heritage;
(3) short-term visitors to another country;
(4) people using an L2 with partners, friends or children;
(5) people using an L2 internationally for specific functions;
(6) people using an L2 internationally for a wide range of functions.

Classroom language learners
(1) Compulsory (immigrants);
(2) Compulsory (education);
(3) Voluntary (education).

Based on Cook[4]

Some parents speak another language with their children, say a home language for children who belong to a minority language group. Some parents use a language with their children that neither of them speaks as a native, for example German in Australia, English in Malaysia or indeed Klingon for one US baby.[9] One common situation is deaf children born to hearing parents, who have to quickly master a sign language to provide for their children's needs. A second language can be an important part of the most intimate relationships. It has always been said that the best way of learning French is to get a boyfriend or girlfriend who is French.

This 'intimate' English is not then something that can be included in the De Swaan hierarchy: it is private and closed. Hence it resembles the L1 genres that people use in close relationships, such as the language addressed to babies, and so is not a public language for use outside the circle of people involved. Hardly anyone sets out to teach it; it is simply acquired by people who find themselves in the appropriate situation. But it is as important to the L2 users in this group as any other L2 use.

(5) *People using an L2 internationally for specific functions.* Many jobs now require the use of a second language. The most obvious is piloting aircraft, where air traffic control uses Aviation English everywhere in the world. The worst-ever air disaster occurred on the ground in Tenerife when a Dutch pilot announced in English *We are now at take off*, meaning he was about to take off, but the Spanish controller understood him to mean that he was waiting at the take-off point at the end of the runway.[10]

Three businessmen on the phone Box 8.4

B: hello Mr Michael
H: is it Barat?
B: yes, how are you sir
H: well I'm OK, but you had to have some er problems with the cheese
B: eeeeeeeerrrrrrr
H: the bad cheese in the customs
B: one minute Mr Akkad will talk with you
H: ok yes
A: Yes Mr Hansen
H: Hello M Akkad we had some informations for you about the cheese with the blowing
A: yes mister Hansen

Firth[11]; *simplified*

Many other worldwide occupations or sports use second languages, whether business, F1 motor racing or call centres. This is a super-central language used for limited purposes across frontiers. L2 users probably use it more than native speakers, who in fact do worse at examinations of Aviation English than L2 users. The community is anybody with a shared specialised interest; the language is a badge of membership or indeed a legal requirement. Restaurants are often places where the staff use a language amongst themselves which is neither their own nor that of the majority community. Waiters in London use Spanish to each other[12]; in Toronto Italian is used behind the scenes in all types of restaurants, regardless of first language.[13] Workers in a Sydney computer firm use Japanese for talking to each other, whether or not they are Japanese. Sometimes these special uses become a variety with its own rules and vocabulary, like the Standard Maritime Communication Phrases set internationally by the International Maritime Organisation in 2001.[14]

The dialogue about cheese in Box 8.4 took place on the phone between three businessmen, one Danish, two Egyptian.[11] A language is being used for negotiation between two non-natives. But is it English? In terms of native speech it seems odd. The cheese was *blowing*? A native couldn't make the noun *information* countable – *some informations* – and wouldn't necessarily know the technical vocabulary for describing cheese so that they could say it was *blowing*; indeed none of the main 32 meanings of *blow* in the *Oxford English Dictionary* appear to apply to cheese.[15] Yet the two men understand each other perfectly. The differences from natives are beside the point.

(6) *People using an L2 internationally for a wide range of functions.* In a sense your first language is up to any demand that you want to place on it – writing a love letter or a cheque, reading a novel or a text message, talking to a spouse or to an audience of 500 people, or defending yourself in court. Many L2 users employ a second language for similar wide-ranging purposes; they are not restricted to specialised functions. Henry VIII used to write love letters to Catherine of Aragon in French; John Dryden composed poems in Latin and translated them into English; the Lennon and McCartney song 'Michelle' codeswitches between English and French.

English has been called the hyper-central language since it may be used virtually anywhere for virtually any reason. At the moment this global usage is often associated with the idea of English as a Lingua Franca (ELF) – English as a global means of communication between native speakers of other languages. ELF has its own grammar and pronunciation, distinct from native speaker English. For instance it does not use the native third person -s in *Rain falls from the sky* and it does not distinguish the native voiced and unvoiced 'th' consonant pair /ð~Θ/ heard in <u>th</u>em/<u>th</u>eme. Box 8.5 lists some of its typical grammatical features.[16]

Features of ELF grammar Box 8.5

- dropping the third person –s: *he like*;
- omitting definite *a/an* and indefinite *the* articles where they are obligatory in native speech, and inserting them where they do not occur in native speech: *He went in car: I like the tea*;
- failing to use 'correct' forms in tag questions. He's right, *isn't it?*
- inserting redundant prepositions, as in *We have to study about physics*;
- overusing certain verbs of high semantic generality, such as *do, have, make, put, take*;
- being over-explicit, as in *black colour* rather than just *black*.

Based on Seidlhofer[16]

So is it actually English that is the hyper-central language or is it ELF? Do people want to acquire something that gets as near as possible to native speech and allows them to speak with natives or do they want a lingua franca that will enable them to talk primarily to other non-natives?

To sum up, talking about L2 users in general is often misleading since they are a large and varied group. There is a big difference between the minds of, say, married couples, businessmen, footballers, pilots, ethnic minority children and tourists. They are not using the second language in the same way; nor have they probably learnt it in the same way. When reading SLA research, one has constantly to ask oneself which L2 user group it is based on.

The largest group of all is missing from this list – *classroom language learners*. These are people who are not so much using the second language in their lives as learning how to use it – in other words learning how to become part of one of the groups of L2 users. For many of these, L2 learning is compulsory. Some need to acquire another language in order to live successfully in an environment where their own first language is not enough. These include not only migrants, expats, businessmen and political refugees, but also speakers of minority languages within the country, say Hispanics in the US.

The compulsory nature of L2 learning is most obvious when it involves legal processes of visas and naturalisation. In Canada immigrants to semi-skilled occupations 'require a level 4 in CLB (Canadian Language Benchmarks) for English or in NCLC' (Niveaux de compétence linguistique canadiens)[17] in French; these are measures of 'communicative proficiency'. UK student visas require an appropriate level in internationally available commercial exams such as Test of English as a Foreign Language (TOEFL)[18] and International English Language Testing System (IELTS).[19] The USA adopts a more informal approach in which an immigration officer assesses the person's ability to speak and to read and write specimen sentences – do not imitate the immigrant who quoted the *Lord of the Rings* sentence *Need brooks no delay, but late is better than never*, to be told *That's not English*. The goal of these people is to join the group that uses the language; it is totally bound up with their lives.

A second group of compulsory L2 learners are those who are forced to study them as part of their education. In most countries all children are required to learn another language, in particular English. Traditionally this occurred at the transition to secondary school at about 12 as in Morocco, but this age is being lowered all the time: in Japan to 10, in Spain to six, in Hong Kong often to three, as we see in Topic 2. To these children a second language is just something on the school curriculum, another subject alongside maths and geography. Whether they are interested in it is another matter. And the goal is the same as that for other subjects – pass the examination at the end and qualify for whatever they want to do at the next stage of their lives. Learning a second language has no immediate or long-term relevance different from any other school subject.

In most European secondary schools outside Ireland and the UK, over 90% of the children are taught English. Universities around the world teach in English, for example in the Netherlands, Saudi Arabia and Hong Kong. These students need to be kept distinct from the L2 user groups above since they are learning the language, not using it for functions other than those of the classroom, even if some may be using it outside. The difference between foreign language learning and second language learning is what lies outside the classroom door, not what happens inside. Most classroom language learning is probably not linked to real future use of the language, whatever teachers may promise. Instead it reflects the need to pass examinations and to get appropriate qualifications: learning another language is simply another school subject, another hurdle to jump.

Sometimes the child's goals for acquiring the first language have been contrasted with those involved in learning a second. Yet a child doesn't really have a goal for learning their first language. They couldn't exist in any normal human environment without language; they just learn language through social environment or because it's built-in to their genes. As Eric Lenneberg once argued, the only requirement for learning a first language is to be a human being.[20] It is pointless to ask why a three-year-old is learning their first language; they are no more aware of it than a fish is aware of the water in which it swims. For the compulsory L2 learners, there is also no choice; they learn a second language or perish, even if perishing only means failing an exam.

The other type of L2 learner is the volunteer student attending evening classes, studying for a modern languages degree or learning online. English university students were questioned about their reasons for learning another language.[1] Box 8.6 shows a handful of the 700 reasons that they came up with and illustrates the diversity of reasons people have for learning a second language. One reason among the 700 is getting a job; another is the stimulating effects of learning another language.

Students' goals in studying another language   Box 8.6

- It's fun and not too difficult.
- Languages are more stimulating than other subjects. There's always something new to learn.
- Languages mean that you can do basically any job that you want anywhere in the world.
- Languages help you to be more open-minded towards other cultures.
- Language learning makes travelling easier, more enjoyable, more enlightening.
- Some languages are beautiful.
- Learning another language shows that you are a hard worker.

Quotations from students interviewed in the Seven Hundred Reasons report[1]

The rationale for much language teaching is to help the students to get into one of the six user groups mentioned above. The aim is to take part in a multilingual community (group 1), visit another country as a tourist (group 2), pilot an aircraft (group 5), or indeed do anything else they want to do in a second language. Any individual will have their own reasons for learning another language; L2 learners are as diverse as any other group of human beings. And of course the strength of language is that it can be used in all sorts of ways that no-one can predict. One of my students was accused by an English newspaper of being a secret police torturer back home, which he denied strenuously; needless to say the course I had taught him did not actually cover police interrogation techniques.

Attitudes to native speakers   Box 8.7

Give your reaction to each of the following statements:

- A person from London speaks English better than a person from Tokyo.   Agree Disagree Don't know

- The person who knows the language best is the native speaker.   Agree Disagree Don't know

- Non-native speakers never speak the language as well as native speakers.   Agree Disagree Don't know

- It is a shame that Ingrid Bergman still had a foreign accent.   Agree Disagree Don't know

- I want to speak a second language like a person from my country, not like a native speaker.   Agree Disagree Don't know

---

Native speakers and L2 users

If you ask L2 learners what they want to become in a second language, the answer is usually none of the groups we have discussed earlier: they want to be native speakers. Students and teachers measure their progress by how close they get to native speakers – an English person aims at speaking French like a French person, say, or at worst admires those who can do so.

How does the second language spoken by L2 users relate to the first language spoken by native speakers? A *native speaker* is usually said to be 'a person who has spoken a certain language since early childhood'. Choose between the answers in Box 8.8 to check your own attitude to this. The results from 400 students of English were that 67% wanted to emulate Student A and be mistaken for native speakers, 32% were like Student B and admired a fluent speaker with a foreign accent.[21]

Which would you rather be? Box 8.8

Student A: I can pronounce English just like a native speaker now. Sometimes people think I am a native speaker.

Student B: I can pronounce English clearly now. Native speakers and non-native speakers understand me wherever I go, but I still have the accent of my country.

Based on Timmis[21]

Like the students, most people seem to believe that the only person who speaks a language properly is a native speaker. But, if the definition above is correct, *no* L2 user could ever become a native speaker: it's far too late. The only ones to make the grade would be children brought up from the very beginning in two languages – early simultaneous bilinguals, who in effect speak two first languages. Students often feel the goal is indeed to speak like a native, or at least to be as close to a native speaker as possible. Consequently most L2 users consider themselves failures for not sounding like native speakers, something they could never be – by definition.

If an L2 user still has a foreign accent or uses non-native grammar, this is usually seen as failure. The novelist Joseph Conrad is often held up as an unsuccessful older L2 user of English (in fact it was his third language, his first being Polish and his second French, which he spoke with 'elegance', 'general ease' and 'no trace of an accent'). According to his fellow novelist Virginia Woolf, he spoke English like 'a foreigner, talking broken English'. A recent radio interview with Dr Frederick Leboyer showed that, at the age of 92, he still had a marked French accent in English. No-one would have mistaken Henry Kissinger, the former US Secretary of State, for anybody other than a German L2 user of English. Measured against native speakers, they are all woefully unsuccessful.

Yet each of them had striking achievements, whether one approves of them or not. Conrad was, and is, highly regarded as an English novelist (providing the major source for *Apocalypse Now* for instance), something few native speakers are capable of. Frederick Leboyer is an international advocate for 'water birthing'. Henry Kissinger fought the Cold War at the highest level of international diplomacy. Their foreign accents were no handicap to their careers in very different fields. Why should they be treated as failed native speakers rather than highly successful L2 users? It doesn't matter if they sound as if they came from Poland, France and Germany rather than Texas, Melbourne or Glasgow. What matters is that they could use their second language efficiently.

What tests measure (quotations)   Box 8.9

- **IELTS (International English Language Testing Scheme, British)**[19]: IELTS band score 9 should not be equated with 'native speaker standard' because the English used by native speakers varies greatly. In fact, score 9 represents an 'Expert User', that is, someone who has fully operational command of the language and makes almost no errors.
- **TOEFL (Test of English as a Foreign Language, USA)**[18]: The TOEFL iBT test measures your ability to use and understand English at the university level. And it evaluates how well you combine your listening, reading, speaking and writing skills to perform academic tasks.
- **CEFR (Common European Framework of Reference for Languages, European)**[22]: Level C2, whilst it has been termed 'Mastery', is not intended to imply native-speaker or near native-speaker competence. What is intended is to characterise the degree of precision, appropriateness and ease with the language which typifies the speech of those who have been highly successful learners.

Most public examination systems now try to express the goal of L2 teaching in other ways than equivalence to native speakers. In Japan the goal is 'Japanese with English abilities', in Israel 'speakers of Hebrew, Arabic or other languages, who can function comfortably in English whenever it is appropriate'. Box 8.9 gives some quotations to show the goals of three well-known schemes for measuring language level. IELTS and TOEFL measure ability to function in English at university, not whether someone is like a native speaker: in other words, English as a super-central language for achieving specific goals. The Common European Framework of Reference for Languages (CEFR) talks of precision, appropriateness and ease, rather than nativeness (and remember that native speakers are often imprecise, inappropriate and hesitant). All three describe a high level of language ability, probably not achieved by most natives. None of them state nativeness as the goal.

A practical example can be seen in the final of the Eurovision song contest in 2013 in which 26 countries competed. Setting aside the two English-speaking countries, UK and Ireland, 16 songs were in English, eight in the language of their country. The Danish song, sung in English, won; the UK entry came 19th and the Irish entry last. Virtually all of the 16 singers had accents that differed markedly from native speakers but this clearly was no drawback for the 600 million who are supposed to have watched some or all of the show.

Nevertheless most SLA researchers, language teachers and students still take it for granted that success in L2 learning means speaking like a native. Two eminent researchers, Hyltenstam and Abramsson,[23] suggest 'absolute native-like command of an L2 may in fact never be possible for any learner', as discussed in Topic 2 – why should it be? A student said 'Non-native speakers need to go the extra mile to speak correctly' – why is native speech the only kind that is correct? Forty-two percent of Chinese students surveyed said they would prefer to speak like a native speaker, but most of them are unlikely to ever meet a native. Language schools sell themselves on the nativeness of their staff. In London one is invited to 'Learn French from the French'; a school in Greece proclaims 'All our teachers are native speakers of English'. In English universities the teachers of modern languages are almost invariably native speakers of the language they teach: 'All languages are taught by native or bi-lingual teachers' proclaims the University of

Essex. Indeed the handsome white male native speaker holding one-to-one classes with students is a major selling point for Japanese private language schools.[24] Some examples of English through romance are seen in Box 8.10.

Japanese women dreaming of native speakers Box 8.10

... since I started to see movies, I used to think 'wow there is a world like this'.

I thought if I need to create a more constant opportunity to actually speak English ... a man.

My mother ... was so excited for me when I told her that he [her new boyfriend] is a classic White English man.

The next time I get a boyfriend I don't want him to speak Japanese!

The reason why I prefer gaijin [foreign] men is because in English I can be my ideal self.

Examples from Takahashi[24]

Yet a native speaker teacher is not a member of any of the L2 user groups the students can aspire to be members of; they never learnt the first language with any particular goal in mind, unlike the L2 students.

François Grosjean has called this a monolingual view of bilingualism: it recognises the only proper use of the language to be that of monolinguals.[25] But the language of L2 users is often different from monolingual native speakers and sometimes richer. Looked at from the monolingual perspective, the L2 user is indeed defective. Japanese L2 users of English seldom learn the 'l~r' contrast in *play* and *pray*. Students from many countries insist on saying *I was interesting in your lecture*, when they mean *I was interested in your lecture*. Recent e-mails to me have started with *Dear Pro. Vivian, Hi Cook, Good morning Vivian, Dear Prof, Respected Dr, Salam Mr Vivian* – and one *Dear Mrs Cook*, a perpetual problem with *Vivian* for non-British speakers, and for many British ones too – the woman's name in the UK is *Vivien* spelled with an 'e'.

So does any of this matter? Only if it stops the message getting across. The 'l~r' contrast can definitely lead to confusion. The polite email openings may, however, work perfectly well for non-native addressees. As an early email adopter, I use no salutation at all: the point of emails was to cut away the antiquated formality of business letters with *Dear X, Best wishes, Yours faithfully*, etc. It is often easier for L2 users to talk to fellow L2 users than to English native speakers. Some trade unionists said that their problems at international meetings conducted in English were not with other L2 users, but with English native speakers, who did not adapt their speech to L2 users.

Looked at from a multilingual perspective, the monolingual is just as defective. Monolinguals can't switch between languages; their awareness of language is poorer; their perceptions of the world are less complex; their command of their first language is worse. Roger Ascham, an advisor to Queen Elizabeth I, said 'For even as a hawk flieth not high with one wing, even so a man reacheth not to excellency with one tongue'.[27] There is nothing wrong with comparing L2 users and native speakers, just as you can compare ducks and geese – they have some similarities and some differences. The problem comes when you set native speakers as the standard and see any similarities of L2 users to monolingual native speaker as success, any differences from native speakers as failure: geese don't make very good ducks because they don't swim very well, etc. The quotation by Chinua Achebe, perhaps the best known Nigerian writer, makes these points very clearly in Box 8.11: L2 users can use the language effectively; they should not try to be like native speakers but should express their own identity through the second language.

Chinua Achebe, 'English and the African writer', 1965 Box 8.11

... my answer to the question: Can an African ever learn English well enough to be able to use it effectively in creative writing? Is certainly yes. If on the other hand you ask: Can he ever learn to use it as a native speaker? I should say. I hope not. It is neither necessary nor desirable for him to be able to do so. The price a world language must be prepared to pay is submission to many different kinds of use. The African writer should aim to use English in a way that brings out his message best without altering the language to the extent that its value as a medium of international exchange will be lost. He should aim at fashioning out an English which is at once universal and able to carry out his peculiar experience.[26]

There are several difficulties with using the monolingual native speaker as the role model for the L2 user. One is that the native speaker is an abstraction. People speaking a first language vary in all sorts of ways. Some are highly educated, some are illiterate. Many speak dialects that vary in grammar, pronunciation and vocabulary. Geordies from Newcastle speak very differently from Londoners, yet Geordies are as much native speakers as those living in London. Which native speaker do you choose?

In actual fact *native speaker* normally means monolingual native speaker of a status variety of the language. In multilingual Switzerland, German-speaking students are not taught Swiss French but Parisian French; French-speaking students are not taught Swiss-German but High German. In the teaching of British English, the target is usually Received Pronunciation (RP) and 'standard grammar'; *you* has the same form for plural and singular; *Newcastle* is pronounced with a long back vowel /ɑ:/; the word for a surface on which you might slip is *slippery*. Geordies however distinguish singular *Thank you* from plural *Thank yous* and pronounce *Newcastle* with an /æ/ vowel; their word for *slippery* is *slippy*. The idealised native speaker target corresponds to a particular minority sub-group of native speakers, not to the totality.

More seriously the native speaker's knowledge of the language is often thought to be identical with the ideal form of the language in grammarbooks. Any grammar normalises a language by excluding non-standard speakers and by including all the vast range of forms found in the language. Native speakers do not know the 263,917 entries and 741,149 meanings in the *Oxford English Dictionary*.[15] It is very dangerous for SLA researchers or language teachers to assume that students need to cover everything in the total description of the language, whether pronunciation, vocabulary or grammar. Measuring the L2 user against the book descriptions of the generalised native speaker weights the odds heavily against them – any actual native speaker wouldn't meet these criteria. If you want to compare an L2 user with a native, then you need to choose an actual native and look at their real speech.

Summary: The native speaker and the L2 user   Box 8.12

- Many L2 learners and L2 users aspire to be as similar as possible to a native speaker. Yet it is hard to pin down what an ideal native speaker might be.
- This native speaker goal cannot be achieved because they already have one language in their minds.
- L2 users and L2 learners need to be assessed against successful L2 users, not against native speakers, as reflected in many contemporary examination systems.

The native speaker is assumed to speak the language perfectly. But, far from being perfect, all native speakers make mistakes – in terms of the standard variety that is. Every time an L2 user makes a mistake, they feel guilty; native speakers seldom notice their own mistakes. On some spelling tasks, L2 users are actually better than monolingual native speakers. A real comparison between L2 users and native speakers would require the comparison of like with like. The native speaker target is a chimera, called by Homer 'a thing of immortal make, not human, lion-fronted and snake behind, a goat in the middle, and snorting out the breath of the terrible flame of bright fire'.

Postscript   Box 8.13

Which goal would you now set for yourself if you were learning a new language? Which L2 user group would you aim to belong to?

Would you accept Graddol's view that native speakers are part of the problem, not the solution?

Further reading

Cook, V.J. (2007) The goals of ELT: Reproducing native-speakers or promoting multi-competence among second language users? In J. Cummins and C. Davison (eds) (2007) *Handbook on English Language Teaching*. New York: Springer, 237–248.

Ortega, L. (2009) *Understanding Second Language Acquisition*. London: Hodder Education.

Scott, V.M. (2009) *Double Talk: Deconstructing Monolingualism in Classroom Second Language Learning*. Boston: Prentice Hall.

References

1. Gallagher-Brett, A. (no date) *Seven Hundred Reasons for Studying Languages*. Southampton: The Higher Education Academy LLAS (Languages, Linguistics, Area Studies), University of Southampton. Online at: www.llas.ac.uk/700reasons. Accessed 21/01/2014.

2. De Swaan, A. (2001) *Words of the World: The Global Language System*. Cambridge: Polity Press.

3. Graddol, D. (2006) *English Next*. London: The British Council. Online at: http://www.britishcouncil.org/learning-research-english-next.pdf

4. Cook, V.J. (2009) Language user groups and language teaching. In V.J. Cook and Li Wei (eds) (2009) *Contemporary Applied Linguistics: Volume 1 Language Teaching and Learning*. London: Continuum, 54–74.

5. Clachar, A. (1997) Ethnolinguistic identity and Spanish proficiency in a paradoxical situation: The case of Puerto Rican return migrants. *Journal of Multilingual and Multicultural Development* 18 (2), 107–124.

6. Gaelic Language Plan (2013) Online at: www.argyll-bute.gov.uk/.../s8462/Mod%20languages%20Document.pdf. Accessed 21/01/2014.

7. Newcastle Mandarin Chinese School (2013) Online at: http://www.newcastlemandarin.org.uk/. Accessed 21/01/2014.

8. Piller, I. (2002) *Bilingual Couples Talk: The Discursive Construction of Hybridity*. Amsterdam: John Benjamins.

9. tvWiki.tv (2006) d'Armond Speers. Online at: http://www.tvwiki.tv/wiki/D%27Armond_Speers

10. Tajima, A. (2004) Fatal miscommunication: English in aviation safety. *World Englishes* 23 (3), 451–470.

11. Firth, A. (1990) Lingua franca negotiations: Towards an interactional approach. *World Englishes* 9, 69–80.

12. Block, D. (2006) *Multilingual Identities in a Global City: London Stories*. London: Palgrave.

13. Norton, B. (2000) *Identity in Language Learning*. Harlow: Longman.

14. International Maritime Organisation (2009) Online at: http://www.imo.org/

15. Oxford University Press (2009) *Oxford English Dictionary*. Online at: http://www.oed.com/

16. Seidlhofer, B. (2004) Research perspectives on teaching English as a lingua franca. *Annual Review of Applied Linguistics* 24, 209–239.

17. *Theoretical Framework for the Canadian Language Benchmarks and Niveaux de compétence linguistique canadiens* (2013) http://www.language.ca/documents/theoretical_framework_web.pdf

18. Educational Testing Services (2013) *The TOEFL iBT Test*. Online at: http://www.ets.org/toefl

19. International English Language Testing System (IELTS) (2009) Online at: http://www.cambridgeenglish.org/exams-and-qualifications/ielts/. Accessed 21/01/2014.

20. Lenneberg, E. (1967) *Biological Foundations of Language*. New York: Wiley & Sons.

21. Timmis, I. (2002) Non-native speaker norms and international English: A classroom view. *English Language Teaching Journal* 56 (3), 240–249.

22. Common European Framework of Reference for Languages (CEF) (2008) Strasburg: Council of Europe. Online at: http://www.coe.int/t/dg4/linguistic/Cadre1_en.asp

23. Hyltenstam, K. and Abrahamsson, N. (2003) Maturational constraints in SLA. In C. Doughty and M. Long (eds) (2003) *The Handbook of Second Language Acquisition.* Oxford: Blackwell, 539–588.

24. Takahashi, K. (2013) *Language Learning, Gender and Desire.* Bristol: Multilingual Matters.

25. Grosjean, F. (2008) *Studying Bilinguals.* Oxford: Oxford University Press.

26. Achebe, C. (1975) The African writer and the English Language. In C. Achebe *Morning Yet on Creation Day.* NY: Anchor Press/Doubleday, 91–103.

27. Ascham, R. (1570) *The Scholemaster.* Printed by Iohn Daye, dwelling ouer Aldersgate.

Epilogue

At this stage the reader probably has the impression of having been treated to a multifarious mish-mash of ideas and approaches, at least in terms of the issues that have been addressed. It is a fact that our journey through the SLA universe has been untroubled by any preoccupation with the logic of the sequence of our halting places. This means, of course, that the chapters can be consumed in any order. It is also true to say that our choice of questions to treat has not been governed by any ideological constraints. The impetus throughout has been to shed light on some of those diverse domains that we ourselves find interesting. Of course, one of the reasons we find them interesting is that we think they are important!

In any case it is clear that second language acquisition research, indeed ALL language acquisition research, is still far from presenting a neat or unified picture of the realities with which it deals. This is because, as each of us has said elsewhere, language acquisition itself is not a monolith. The phenomenon of language acquisition, and second language acquisition in particular, is immensely complex and, it seems, unendingly multifaceted. It cannot be explained in terms of a single theoretical perspective – at least not one that has been hit on so far. SLA researchers are obliged, and may always be obliged, to deal with the problems and mysteries that lie before them in this area, making use of a vast array of different insights and research approaches.

In other words answers free of complications are rare. Indeed, with the growing influence of dynamic systems and complexity theory thinking in the field, the prospect of answers free of complications grows ever more remote! This applies to 'basic research' issues, such as the relationship between the languages in the L2 user's mind or the nature and effects of the maturational factor in L2 development, but it also applies (even more so if anything!) to the language teaching implications of SLA research. What chances, then, are there for teachers to benefit from the whole SLA research enterprise?

We have suggested that SLA research needs to take the conundrums of the language classroom much more explicitly into consideration in framing its investigative programmes. Even as things stand, however, there are numerous avenues for teachers and learners to explore when, for example, the learners fail to learn what the teachers teach. Questions to explore in such circumstances include, for instance: whether motivation is low in regard to coming to grips with (some aspects of) the target language; whether there is some cross-linguistic impediment to the ready internalisation of (some aspects of) the target language; whether the learners are developmentally 'ready' for the target structures/items being presented to them; or whether there is an input problem in terms of the frequency of exposure to the target structures/items concerned. In all of these the findings of SLA research can help.

Of course, the outcome of such probing is unlikely to be a set of straightforward solutions. As Oscar Wilde famously put it, the truth is rarely pure and never simple! Each learner in a class may be found to be associated with his/her particular mix of responses to questions such as those above, or there may be clusters of response-types across different groups. But at least with modern pedagogy – group-work, pair-work, project-work, learner autonomy building, etc. – there is the hope of being able to cope with such variation as teaching increasingly tries to treat learners as individuals. If the process begins with the posing of relevant questions and continues by drawing freely on the full armoury of pedagogical notions and strategies that has accumulated over the years, some possibility exists of making progress in the struggle towards more effective teaching and learning.

SLA research, if it does nothing else, asks the right questions; and our little book, if it does nothing else, may give some useful guidance as to what some of those questions are.

Key Topics Glossary

acculturation: the processes whereby members of one cultural group do or do not adopt the perspectives and behaviour patterns of another.

audiolingual method of language teaching: originating in the USA in the early 1940s, this made students repeat sentences recorded on tape and practice structures in repetitive drills. Its peak of popularity was the 1960s, though it was not much used in British-influenced EFL.

audio-visual method of language teaching: this emerged chiefly in France in the 1960s and 1970s and was a strong influence on modern language teaching in England. Visual images were used to show the meaning of spoken dialogues through film-strips and taped dialogues for repetition; no written language was used.

authentic speech: 'an authentic text is a text that was created to fulfil some social purpose in the language community in which it was produced'. Little, D., Devitt, S. & Singleton, D. (1988). *Authentic Texts in Foreign Language Teaching: Theory and Practice*. Dublin: Authentik.

behaviourism: a movement in 20th century psychology originating from John Watson that saw language learning as a mechanical process of associating stimuli and responses, applied to language by Robert Lado and others and associated with audiolingualism.

bilingual/bilingualism: varying definitions going from perfect command of two languages to the ability to use another language for practical purposes, however trivial the use.

character: the name for a single symbol of a writing system such as Chinese, i.e. 人 ('person') is a character. The term is also used in computing for any distinct symbol such as the letter <a>, number <6> or other form <@>.

classifiers: some languages like Japanese have classifiers for counting objects (*koko ni issatsu no hon ga aru* (literally 'here is one-classifier book') to show what kind of object is involved rather than articles, resembling the English phrases for counting uncountables, *a glass of water*, *a pile of sand*, etc.

codeswitching: the ability of many bilinguals to switch language in mid-conversation or mid-sentence when talking to people who know both languages.

communicative competence: the speaker's ability to put language to communicative use, usually traced back to Dell Hymes. Chomsky uses the more inclusive term *pragmatic competence*.

communicative language teaching: this bases teaching on the students' need to communicate, originally seen as the functions that the second language had for them and the meanings they wanted to express, perhaps the most influential approach to teaching around the globe since the 1970s, in a great variety of forms.

compound bilinguals: the bilingual's two languages are related via a common underlying set of concepts.

content words: content words such as nouns, verbs and adjectives have lexical meaning, invariable stress pattern and form, and are usually three letters long or longer.

Contrastive Analysis (CA): an approach to SLA research that starts by comparing the first and second languages and uses the resulting differences and similarities to predict the problems that L2 learners face.

coordinate bilinguals: the bilingual's two languages are distinct both in form and in terms of underlying concepts.

critical period hypothesis (CPH): the claim that the human capacity to learn language declines radically after a particular age, originating from Eric Lenneberg.

English as Lingua Franca (ELF): the version of English spoken by non-native speakers to each other internationally, with its own grammar and conventions.

font: strictly a complete set of type for printing, nowadays mostly referring to a particular design for the whole set of characters available through a computer keyboard, called by typographers a *typeface*.

function (structure) words: words that have a grammatical function such as articles *the/a*, prepositions *to/in* and pronouns *I/her*, typically variable in spoken form and written abbreviations (*have*, *'ve*; *is*, *'s*) and in English having three or less letters. Visit YouTube: http://www.youtube.com/watch?v=R7mTjOifoVo

grammar: the system of relationships between elements of the sentence that links the 'sounds' of language to the 'meanings', used both for the knowledge of language in a speaker's mind, and for the system written down in rules, grammar books and the like. Conventionally syntax refers to grammar above the level of the word, morphology to grammar below the level of the word.

grammar translation method of language teaching: the traditional 'classical' academic style of teaching which makes heavy use of grammar explanation and translation as teaching techniques.

grammatical (linguistic) competence: the native speaker's knowledge of language, i.e. language as a mental possession.

grammatical morphemes: a collective term for morphemes that play a role in the grammar of the sentence, such as the articles *the/to*, prepositions *to/in*, or inflections such as the past tense *-ed*, *liked* or the possessive *''s' John's*.

grammatical system: a term within Hallidayan linguistics in which 'the grammar is seen as a network of interrelated meaningful choices', for example articles.

hierarchy of languages: the language hierarchy (De Swaan) goes from peripheral (local) like Finnish, to central like English in India, to super-central like French used across several countries for limited reasons, to hyper-central like English used globally for any reason.

inflections: a grammatical system of showing meaning by changing word endings, as in the English *–ed* past tense inflection, *I looked*, absent from some languages like Vietnamese or Chinese.

instrumental motivation: learning the language for a career goal or other practical reason.

integration continuum: the relationship of the languages in a community or a mind on a continuum between total integration and total separation.

integrative motivation (integrativeness): learning the language in order to take part in the culture of its people.

interlanguage: the learner's linguistic system as a grammar in its own right rather than as a defective version of the target language.

intonation: significant changes of pitch during speech, used in English to convey some emotional and grammatical meanings, but in tone languages like Chinese to convey lexical meaning, i.e. differences between words, in a similar way to differences between phonemes. Visit YouTube: http://www.youtube.com/watch?v=_HGxfR7Sziw

letter/sound correspondences: in sound-based scripts, written symbols like letters correspond to sounds of the spoken language, sometimes simply as in 'phonetic' scripts like Italian, sometimes in complex and indirect ways as in English.

linguistico-cultural identity: the perceived identity of an individual or group in terms of belonging to, being affiliated to, a particular language community and culture.

mental lexicon: speakers of a language store the words and word-related elements (e.g. fixed expressions) they know in a mental dictionary or lexicon containing many thousands of items.

mnemonic strategy: conscious attempts to memorise items, for instance through key words.

mode: L2 users may be either in bilingual mode in which both languages are equally available to them or in monolingual mode in which only one is active, whether first or second, an idea introduced by François Grosjean.

morpheme: the smallest meaningful grammatical unit, either a word in its own right – *cook* – or part of a word – *cooks ('-s'), cooker (-er)*.

morphology: grammar dealing with items smaller than the word such as word-formation (*hat-rack*) and inflections (*'s, -ing,- ed*, etc.).

motivation: the impetus to create and sustain intentions and goal-seeking acts.

multi-competence: the overall system of a mind or a community that uses more than one language.

multilingual/multilingualism: countries or individuals that use more than one language for everyday purposes.

native speaker: a person speaking the first language they learnt as a child, typically taken to be a 'prestige' standard variety.

parameters: in post-1981 Chomskyan syntax, differences between languages are captured by setting the value for a small number of parameters, like a row of light switches each set to on or off.

phoneme: the distinctive sounds of a particular language system are its phonemes, studied in phonology. Thus in English the sounds /p/ and /b/ are different phonemes because they distinguish /pʌn/ *pun* from /bʌn/ *bun*.

phonetic script: a way of transcribing the sounds of language accurately through an agreed set of phonetic symbols, commonly the International Phonetic Alphabet (IPA).

phonetics: the sub-discipline of linguistics that studies the production and perception of the actual speech sounds themselves, distinct from phonology.

phonology: the area of linguistics that studies the sound systems of particular languages, contrasting with phonetics.

pro-drop parameter (null subject parameter): a parameter in Chomskyan syntax; languages set this either to pro-drop in which the subject of the sentence may be left out, as in Italian *Sono di Torino* (am from Turin) and Chinese *Shuo* (speak), or to non-pro-drop in which the subject must be present in the actual sentence as in English, German and French.

punctuation: conventional marks in addition to the main letters or characters of the script, either to aid reading aloud or to clarify grammatical structure.

reverse transfer: carrying over aspects of the second language to the first.

RP: The prestige accent of British English is known by the two letters RP, originally standing for 'Received Pronunciation'. It is spoken in all regions of the UK, albeit by a small minority of speakers.

second language (L2): 'A language acquired by a person in addition to his mother tongue' UNESCO. Often covers third and later languages.

second language (L2) learner: someone who is learning another language but not using it every day, i.e. students in class.

second language (L2) user: someone who knows and uses a second language at any level, as opposed to a second language learner. Visit YouTube: http://www.youtube.com/watch?v=22b4o8N9tao

structuralist linguistics: a method of describing language as sets of structures by e.g. Leonard Bloomfield, to be learnt by stimulus and response, applied to language teaching by Robert Lado and Nelson Brooks, leading to the audiolingual method.

task-based learning: a teaching method in which learning arises from particular tasks the students do in the classroom.

Universal Grammar: sometimes Universal Grammar refers simply to the aspects of language that all languages have in common. In the Chomskyan sense, Universal Grammar refers to the language faculty built in to the human mind, which allows everyone to learn a human language.

word order: the main aspect of word order is the order of subject, verb and object, which varies between languages. Another word order variation is whether prepositions come before nouns – *in New Orleans* – or postpositions after nouns – *Nippon ni* (Japan in).

writing system: 'A set of visible or tactile signs used to represent units of language in a systematic way ...': [sense 1] 'the basic types of graphic systems designed to represent language ...'; [sense 2]'. Coulmas, F. (1996). *The Blackwell Encyclopaedia of Writing System*. Oxford: Blackwell. p.56.

A more extensive glossary is online at: http://homepage.ntlworld.com/vivian.c/Linguistics/LinguisticsGlossary.htm

Index

Numbers in bold refer to the page where the expression is explained in the glossary.